BI 35033169

KT-174-839

The Essential Guide to
Using ICT Creatively in the Primary Classroom

The Essential Guide to Using ICT Creatively in the Primary Classroom

Steve Woods

Longman
is an imprint of

BIRMINGHAM CITY
LIBRARY
UNIVERSITY

Harlow, England • London • New York • Boston • San Francisco • Toronto • Sydney • Singapore • Hong Kong
Tokyo • Seoul • Taipei • New Delhi • Cape Town • Madrid • Mexico City • Amsterdam • Munich • Paris • Milan

PEARSON EDUCATION LIMITED

Edinburgh Gate
Harlow CM20 2JE
Tel: +44 (0)1279 623623
Fax: +44 (0)1279 431059
Website: www.pearsoned.co.uk

BIRMINGHAM CITY UNIVERSITY
Book no 3503369
Subject 572.133466 Woo
LIBRARY

First published in Great Britain in 2010

© Pearson Education 2010

The right of Steve Woods to be identified as author of this work has been asserted by him in accordance with the Copyright, Designs and Patents Act 1988.

Pearson Education is not responsible for the content of third party internet sites.

ISBN: 978-1-4082-2497-7

British Library Cataloguing-in-Publication Data
A catalogue record for this book is available from the British Library

Library of Congress Cataloging-in-Publication Data
Woods, Steve.
  The essential guide to using ICT creatively in the primary classroom / Steve Woods.
    p. cm.
  Includes index.
  ISBN 978-1-4082-2497-7 (pbk.)
  1. Visual literacy--Study and teaching (Primary) 2. Education, Elementary--Activity programs.
  3. Language arts (Primary) 4. Reading (Primary) 5. English language--Composition and
  exercises--Study and teaching (Primary) I. Title.
  LB1523.W64 2010
  372.133'4--dc22
                              2010002737

All rights reserved. No part of this publication may be reproduced, stored in a retrieval system, or transmitted in any form or by any means, electronic, mechanical, photocopying, recording or otherwise, without either the prior written permission of the publisher or a licence permitting restricted copying in the United Kingdom issued by the Copyright Licensing Agency Ltd, Saffron House, 6–10 Kirby Street, London EC1N 8TS. This book may not be lent, resold, hired out or otherwise disposed of by way of trade in any form of binding or cover other than that in which it is published, without the prior consent of the publisher.

10 9 8 7 6 5 4 3 2 1
14 13 12 11 10

Typeset in 11/14 pt ITC Stone Sans by 30
Printed and bound in Great Britain by Henry Ling Ltd, Dorchester, Dorset

The publisher's policy is to use paper manufactured from sustainable forests.

Contents

About the author

Steve Woods started his teaching career as a classroom teacher in a large inner city primary school. After 10 years' experience he became the primary ICT advisory teacher for his Local Education Authority. Currently he is a consultant teacher for ICT, supporting both teachers and students within over 100 primary and secondary schools in the North West.

Publisher's acknowledgements

We are grateful to the following for permission to reproduce copyright material:

Screenshot on page 82 from ArtRage 2. Used with the permission of Ambient Design Ltd; Screenshots on pages 37, 38, 39 used with the permission of Dr Karl Harrison; Screenshot on page 37 from Merton College, Oxford. The Warden and Fellows of Merton College Oxford. Drawn by Jeremy Bays, www.art-work-shop.co.uk; Screenshots on pages 24, 28 and 34 from Nokiddin.co.uk; Screenshots on pages 102 and 103 from Partners in Rhyme; Screenshots on pages 61, 62, 63 and 64 from Scratch. Scratch is developed by the Lifelong Kindergarten Group at the MIT Media Lab. See http://scratch.mit.edu; Screenshots from pages 26, 27 and 32 from Smart Technologies. © 2007-2010, SMART Technologies ULC. All rights reserved.

Audacity® software is copyright © 1999-2010 Audacity Team. The name Audacity® is a registered trademark of Dominic Mazzoni.

Microsoft screen shots reprinted with permission from Microsoft Corporation.

Many thanks to Jane Woods for allowing us to use her photographs.

In some instances we have been unable to trace the owners of copyright material, and we would appreciate any information that would enable us to do so.

Introduction

To teach using ICT a few essentials need to be in place. Everything needs to work and the teacher needs to know how the technology they are introducing will move pupils forward. This sounds simple, but the final essential factor is time (something that the modern classroom practitioner is very short of).

The aim of this book is to reduce the time you need to spend preparing lessons that involve ICT and also to introduce you to a way of teaching that will appeal to the digital natives that inhabit your classroom.

This book will answer the questions that you feel silly asking. What is a Dongle? What is the difference between Save and Save As? Which wire goes where? I then move on to give step-by-step guides to getting started with the most popular freeware applications (freeware is software that is free to download and use).

In the creative projects chapter I relate the freeware (you have just learned to use) to curriculum-based creative projects that can be lifted straight from the book or adapted easily to fit in with whatever you are teaching. Wherever possible, I have shown where these projects can fit in with current QCA documentation. However, these ideas are generic and will work alongside any scheme you are currently using.

If you are looking to refresh your school curriculum, improve yourself professionally or are just searching for something new to inspire your class then this book will first guide you through some of the basics, then take you and your pupils on an exciting and enjoyable learning journey.

There is no doubt in my mind that ICT is likely to be involved in the future careers of 99 per cent, if not all of the pupils you are currently teaching. I believe that the more technology you are immersed in the easier it is to use, a prime example is the way the children we teach today use mobile phones. Ask any pupil in your school what their phone does and they will probably forget to tell you that it makes calls and sends texts. It will most probably be a picture taking, video making, internet surfing, MP3 playing, all-singing, all-dancing device. Today's children are using technology 24 hours a day. Games are online, they web chat with friends, create blogs and web pages, and then come to school and switch off. To really enthuse the children we teach, we need to enter their world, and ICT is an ideal vehicle of choice.

> 'We are preparing our children for jobs that don't exist yet using technology that hasn't been invented to solve problems that we don't even know are problems yet.'

> (Karl Fisch, *Shift Happens*, 2006)

The inspiration for this book has come from actually doing projects, similar to these in the creative projects chapter, in the classroom. I hope this book will inspire you to look at the way you deliver, record and evaluate your lessons and, most of all, make ICT easier for you and better for your pupils.

Going further

Fisch, K. (2006) *Shift Happens* (PowerPoint presentation at Arapahoe High School, Colorado)

Part
1

The basics

Introduction

Your school technician is in great demand, you wait for days to get something fixed (that they say is simple), but when they explain it to you they might as well be speaking another language. Does this seem familiar? The following chapters aim to take you through some of the basics needed for general day-to-day teaching and keeping your classroom computer up and running.

Where do all the wires go?

What this chapter will explore:

- The different wires, cables and plugs you are likely to encounter in the classroom
- The main hardware problems teachers face and how to overcome them
- Setting up and troubleshooting common problems

Where do all the wires go?

Wires are an essential part of letting your computer communicate, send and receive power. There are lots of different types, and each has a different function in the classroom. If you understand their functions and properties you will feel more confident when connecting new and existing equipment. However, even though reading this chapter will make you more self-sufficient, note that, no matter what level of IT skills a person has, everyone ends up with a giant knot of cable spaghetti around their classroom computer!

There are numerous cables and each type has its own specific place to connect. The good news is that designers have given different types different connectors. A good rule to live by is: 'If it fits in the hole it's in the correct place'.

Note: The next section of this chapter is designed to be a reference for the times when you acquire a new piece of equipment. You may have heard the phrase 'plug and play' – most wires can be plugged in while your machine is running but some need to be removed in a particular way. If you are unsure of what to do, it is safer to shut your computer down before removing any cables.

USB cable (Universal Serial Bus): This is a cable that allows a number of different **peripheral devices** to connect in a standardised way. The end that connects to the computer is always the same, but there are a number of different connectors for the other end, which depend on the device being connected.

USB cable, PC end

USB cable, device end

USB socket

USB cables can require a substantial amount of power from your computer to work. You should always 'safely remove' a device connected by USB to stop any damage or loss of data. Close the programs using the device and follow the diagram below for safe removal.

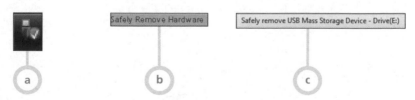

a. Hover over this icon in the Notification Area.

b. A 'Safely Remove Hardware' pop-up appears. Left-click it.

c. Select the device to remove. You will receive a message when it is safe to remove it. If you receive a message that the device can not be stopped, it is good practice to wait until your computer is shut down before removing.

Note: If the symbol is not there the device may already have been removed (turning a digital camera off can be the same as safely removing).

Ethernet cable: Connects your computer to both the internet and the school network (you may not have one if your school uses a **wireless network**).

Ethernet cable

Ethernet socket

SD card (Secure Digital): Widely used in digital cameras, mobile phones and devices that need to be small, this 'solid state' card provides a secure and durable method of storage.

SD card

Microphone jack: A microphone commonly has a 1.5mm **jack** and usually plugs into a pink socket with a microphone symbol next to it. The microphone socket is a mono socket. Although most modern laptops have a built-in microphone, a wired microphone may make it easier, especially if you have younger children, for your class to make recordings, as it will allow them to hold the microphone close to their mouths to get a clear input.

Microphone jack

TOP TIP!

Holding the microphone below your mouth so it is touching your chin can eliminate a lot of popping and breathing noises.

Headphones jack: The headphones jack is similar to the microphone jack. It usually goes into a green or black socket with a headphones symbol.

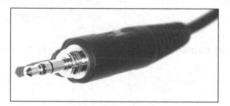

Headphones jack

Sound sockets: The sound sockets on a computer are usually arranged in a row as shown.

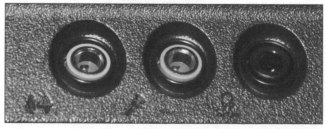

Sound sockets

FireWire: Similar to the USB cable, FireWire is a serial bus communication developed for high-speed/real-time data transfer. You are most likely to come across FireWire in school when using a high-quality video editing suite. FireWire allows you to control the camera from the computer and watch the video scenes you are capturing.

FireWire cable, PC end   FireWire cable, device end

Dongle: The first dongles were created to authenticate software to stop illegal copying. Nowadays a dongle is a small peripheral device that connects to your computer, usually into the USB port. You may have a storage device, a Bluetooth connector or a wireless internet dongle for your computer.

Dongle

Interactive whiteboard: An interactive whiteboard will certainly be an item you already are (or shortly will be) connecting to your computer. Modern boards have a USB connection, whereas older boards use **parallel pin** connectors. These boards are basically a giant mouse. Whether you can use your finger or need a pen to control them they will allow you to control the functions of your computer mouse in a manner that can greatly assist creative and interactive teaching with ICT. Some of the latest boards allow users to attach **pen drives** to show images and incorporate projector control functions and other shortcuts.

What's wrong and how do I fix it?

Setting up, common problems and fixes

Although the diagrams below show a laptop, this section is a generic guide for setting up almost any computer in the classroom. It is assumed that the computer is working and all cables you may need are present. The diagram shows the cable and the socket it connects to. These will be in different places on different models of machine, but will look the same.

Setting up a laptop in the classroom

Start with the computer switched off. Only when everything is connected should you turn it on – this will allow everything you have connected to be automatically detected, and save you time in the long run.

There is no need to tighten these screws unless the cable keeps falling out

Connect the VGA cable

Connect the Ethernet cable (unless you are wireless)

Connect your board (most interactive boards have a USB connection)

It is also a good idea to connect to the power supply rather than use the battery

Connect sound (usually a jack plug but can be a USB)

Switch on the projector or display device (you may have a large LCD screen instead).

Finally, turn the computer on. Remember that on some machines you will need to wait until you are fully logged on before you see the display on your board.

TOP TIP!

Once your machine is working, colour code the connections with stickers to help you quickly identify them again.

Although it is generally preferable to get an expert to fix your ICT problems, a lot of schools do not have a dedicated technician and in some cases they only visit as little as once every fortnight. The table below contains some of the most commonly encountered ICT problems and gives advice on how to fix them. If the fix does not work then you should contact your technician.

Table of common problems and their fixes

Problem	Fix
No internet	Check your Ethernet cable is plugged in or, if you have a **wireless connection**, make sure it is activated on your computer. Also, check if others have the internet – if it is not working in other rooms then it is not your connections at fault.
The projector is not showing my screen	Check your **VGA** cable is plugged in. Check your projector is switched on. Check the projector is set to VGA or computer input (this will be on the remote). On a laptop there is a key to press to use dual screen (normally F4 or F5). There is usually a picture of a screen on the button – consult your manual if unsure.
No sound	Check you have the speaker cable in the correct socket (it is usually green or has a picture of headphones next to it). Check the speakers are on and have power. Check the volume is up on your machine. Check the system volume (double-click the speaker icon in the system tray).
DVD will not play	Open the DVD **drive** and close it again (the DVD should play automatically). Go to My Computer and double-click the DVD drive. Check you have a program that will play DVDs. Try it on another machine.
Board not interactive	Most boards have indicator lights to show an active connection – check they are on. If you have a USB connection, unplug it, wait for 10 seconds and plug it back in again. If persistent restart your computer. →

Table of common problems and their fixes (continued)

Problem	Fix
Can not see shared drive	Check your Ethernet/wireless connection as well as the internet – this connection also connects you to the school network.
When I write on the SmartBoard it disappears	If you pick up a pen and write it will stay until you put the pen down and touch the board. If you want to keep what you have written, click on the camera in the top right corner and it will capture to SmartNotebook.
I can not print	Check the printer has no flashing lights, and has ink and paper. Press Ctrl+P and check you are sending the job to the correct printer (you may be printing in a different room). If there is a printer icon in the system tray, double-click it, cancel all print jobs and send your printing again.

Why not try this?

Next time you have a problem that you have to ask the technician to fix, ask them to explain what has happened and why. Don't be afraid to keep asking 'why?' if you do not understand. Remember, you will be saving yourself and them time in the future.

Key ideas summary

Learning to support yourself in the classroom is like learning a second language, it is only once you make the effort to talk to real local people (the technicians) that you make progress. Only then do you begin to truly understand the foreign words you are learning (computer jargon) and benefit from your efforts.

Building a solid foundation – essential computer skills

What this chapter will explore:

- Saving and finding work
- Cut, Copy and Paste, including how and when to apply them
- The Taskbar and its classroom functions
- Hyperlinking
- Using pictures from the internet

All great structures rely on solid foundations. Classroom ICT is no exception. Knowing the basics and how to apply them when faced with different situations is essential to good classroom practice.

Saving and finding work

Saving is easy but finding your work again can sometimes be difficult. An understanding of file structure is key to saving and then finding your work.

Any piece of information you create is referred to as a file when you save it. When you save a file you are asked to give it a name and specify where you want it to go.

In an office you would first put a file in a folder and then put the folder in a common place where it could be found again, i.e. a filing cabinet. In the same way, all information on a computer is stored on devices called drives. Drives can be fixed storage, e.g. your hard drive/s (they are fixed inside your computer), or removable storage, e.g. CD, DVD, USB storage (they can be removed and passed between systems). All of these drives are given a letter and that letter helps both you and the programs on your computer to locate them.

Here is the most common setup: the letter C is allocated to the main hard drive (called the C: drive). The C: drive holds all of the programs that run your computer. These programs do not take up all of the space on the C: drive. The extra space can be used to store your personal files and any extra programs you might want to use.

To help organise the C: drive, folders can be created. Your computer will come with some folders already in place: such as My Documents, My Pictures, My Music, etc. These folders are all sections of the C: drive.

Let's look at it in terms of your school. The whole building is the C: drive. The classrooms are folders inside the C: drive. The children and staff are the files. The classrooms (folders) are named, for example 'Mr Woods' class', and the staff and children (files) are allocated to the correct classrooms. If a new child arrives (file created) they are put into the correct class (saved to the correct folder).

Whenever you click File > Save you will see a dialog box similar to the one at the top of the page opposite. Follow these steps each time you save a file to ensure that you can find it again.

a. Click on My Documents.

b. Do you need to create a folder? If yes go to c, if no go to d.

c. Click on the Create New Folder button. The New Folder dialog box will open as shown. Type in a name for your folder, then click OK.

d. Type a file name here and click Save.

Using File > Save

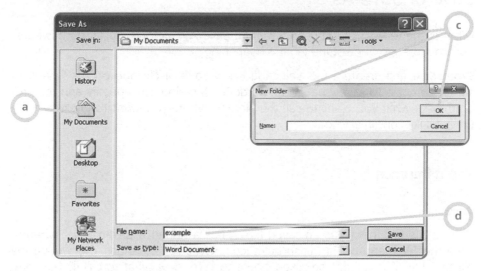

Your file will be in your My Documents folder or inside a folder you created inside the My Documents folder. To find it, click on Start and Documents (if you are using Windows 7) or My Documents (if using XP). Below is an example of my, My Documents folder:

Name	Date modified	Type	Size	Tags
Creativity	19/07/2008 18:53	File Folder		
DT	19/07/2008 18:51	File Folder		
English	19/07/2008 18:50	File Folder		
Geography	19/07/2008 18:51	File Folder		
History	19/07/2008 18:51	File Folder		
ICT	19/07/2008 18:52	File Folder		
Ideas	19/07/2008 18:53	File Folder		
Maths	19/07/2008 18:51	File Folder		
My Music	19/07/2008 18:52	File Folder		
My Pictures	19/07/2008 18:52	File Folder		
Newsletters	19/07/2008 18:52	File Folder		
Reports	19/07/2008 18:52	File Folder		
Science	19/07/2008 18:51	File Folder		

Why not try this?

Spend some time organising your documents on your hard drive. Set up new folders and subfolders to help you save and find new documents quickly and easily.

Save or Save As

What is the difference between Save and Save As? Before you tackle this question you need to understand what is happening.

When you first create a file, selecting File > Save or clicking on the Save icon starts a process to save what you have done. A dialog box appears and the program asks what you want to call the file and where you want to put it (see the previous section on saving).

The difference

Save

Once a file has initially been saved (i.e. it has a name), clicking Save, whether from the File menu or via the shortcut icon, saves your changes, overwriting the existing file. You will not be asked where to save to or what to call it. The computer assumes that you want to use the original settings.

Example: I make a worksheet for my class in Word. I save it to My Documents and call it 'worksheet'. I notice that I have missed some punctuation, so I make the changes and click the Save icon. The changes overwrite the original, so the worksheet is saved with the corrected punctuation. The file is still called 'worksheet' and is still in My Documents.

Save As

Save As (click File > Save As) allows you to change where you want to save a file and also its name. This allows a second version of the file to be made (Note: It can not have the same name if you want it in the same folder as the original.)

Example: I make a worksheet for my class in Word. I save it to My Documents and call it 'worksheet'. I decide to make a few changes to the worksheet to make it suitable for the less able group. I make the changes and click File > Save As. I keep it in My Documents but change the file name to 'worksheet less able'. Now I have two versions, the original and the modified worksheet.

> **TOP TIP!**
>
> *Nearly all programs have an icon on the toolbar that allows you to save. For example, in a Word document it is a picture of a floppy disk near the top left corner.*

Cut, Copy and Paste

Before you learn about the three tools that you will probably use most frequently, I would like to take a moment to explain how they work.

Your computer has a piece of memory known as the **Clipboard**. This will remember anything you ask it to, but it usually only remembers one thing at a time. Practically every program on your computer will allow you to **cut**, **copy** and **paste** text, pictures or objects as long as you can select or **highlight** them. The Cut, Copy and Paste commands are found in the Edit tab on all programs that allow them.

- **Cut**: This command cuts a previously highlighted text, object or picture out (so you won't see it any more) and holds it in the Clipboard. It will stay there and can be pasted as many times as you like until you cut or copy something else (it only holds one thing at a time).

- **Copy**: This command copies a previously highlighted text, object or picture (it will not disappear from the work area) so you can paste it again as many times as you like until you cut or copy something else.

- **Paste**: This command pastes what you have cut or copied to wherever you have selected.

The main ways to cut, copy and paste

If you have not used these tools before, here they are in their simplest form. In the figure below, I am going to cut, copy and paste within a Word Document.

Cut

a. Highlight the text. Left-click (hold) and drag the cursor across the text you want to cut.

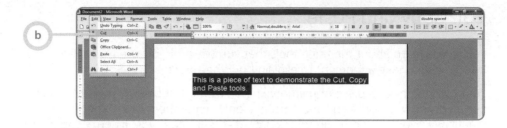

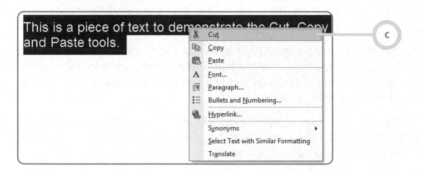

b. Click Edit > Cut, or press Ctrl+X (hold down Ctrl and press X).

c. Alternatively, right-click on the selected text and select Cut from the menu that appears.

Copy

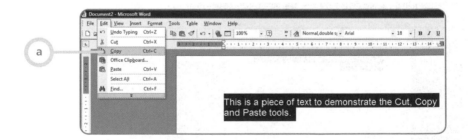

a. To copy, highlight the text and click Edit > Copy, or press Ctrl+C (i.e. hold down Ctrl and press C).

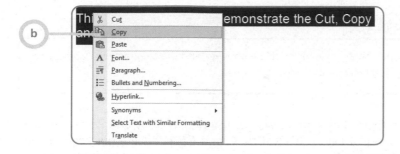

b. Alternatively, right-click on the selected text and choose Copy from the menu that appears.

c. The text is now held in the Clipboard. If you have cut the text you will no longer see it. If you have used Copy it will remain on screen.

Paste

Note: To paste you must have previously cut or copied so there is something in the Clipboard memory to paste.

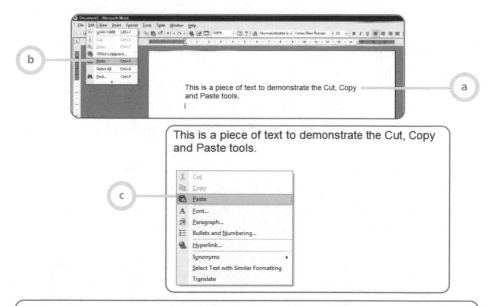

a. First deselect the text by clicking at the end of the sentence. Then press Enter so the cursor is on a new line below the text.

b. Select Edit > Paste to paste, or press Ctrl+V (hold down Ctrl and press V).

c. Alternatively, right-click below the text and select Paste from the menu that appears.

Why not try this?

Practise using all three ways of cutting, copying and pasting outlined above and see which way you feel most comfortable with.

Note: Although there is no correct way of using Cut, Copy and Paste, I believe that using the shortcut keys (Ctrl+X, Ctrl+C and Ctrl+V) is the quickest and will be using this method in the rest of the book. The only time I would not use the shortcut keys would be if I was using an Interactive Whiteboard with the keyboard out of reach or in a position where it would take more time to use the shortcut keys than the other methods.

TOP TIP!

You can also copy from one program to another. This can be found at the end of the next section on the Taskbar, as it is an integral part of the process.

The Taskbar

The **Taskbar** is found at the bottom of your computer screen and has three essential parts that you will need to use in your classroom:

- the Start button, where you can 'start' any program, file or folder on your system;
- the tasks, buttons that represent open programs – clicking on these will allow you to switch between them;
- the Notification Area, a series of icons that allow you to quickly launch programs and check on the status of your computer, i.e. battery life, time, date, etc.

The Taskbar

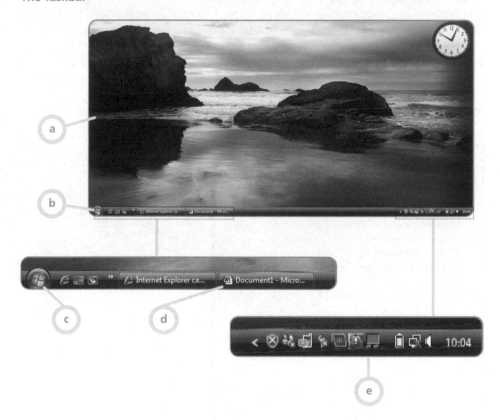

a. This is the desktop, the screen you see when you switch on.

b. The Taskbar.

c. The Start button. Click on this to open all the programs, files and folders on the computer.

d. The Taskbar shows two programs running. Clicking on these buttons allows you to work within that program.

e. The Notification Area. This contains icons to give statistics (e.g. battery life and the time) and also contains 'quick launch' icons for programs.

To ensure you get the most out of your Taskbar when using your computer in conjunction with an interactive whiteboard it is wise to make sure that 'Auto Hide' is not activated. This is a setting that causes the Taskbar to disappear until you hover the cursor near it. There is nothing wrong with having this setting, but when working interactively it can reduce the pace of a lesson. This will only need to be done once but, if you use different computers, may be useful to remember.

Switching off Auto Hide

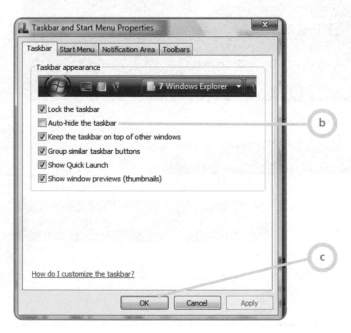

a. Right-click on a blank part of the Taskbar. You will see a dialog box similar to this.

b. Make sure Auto Hide the Taskbar is unchecked.

c. Click OK.

Once you understand the Taskbar, using multiple programs and switching between them is simple.

Why not try this?

Try opening two programs to practise. In the figure at the top of the page opposite I have opened a Word document and Internet Explorer.

The Taskbar in the classroom

a. To switch to Internet Explorer click on this button on the Taskbar and it will open.

b. If you want to work on the Word document instead, click on its button on the Taskbar and it will open.

TOP TIP!

Opening programs brings a lull to a lesson where pupils can switch off. To increase the pace of a lesson that uses the interactive whiteboard, before the lesson starts open the programs you will be using and minimise them (see the figure on minimising and maximising). Now your pupils can not see what is coming next and you can select the programs on the Taskbar, rather than having to wait for them to open.

Minimise and maximise

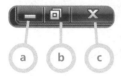

a. Minimise to a button on the Taskbar.

b. Maximise to full screen or restore down to a smaller window.

c. Close the program.

Copying and pasting between programs

The Taskbar can also be used to copy from one program to another. Overleaf is an example of using the Taskbar to copy from an internet page to a Word document something that will save you time making worksheets and other resources.

Copying between programs

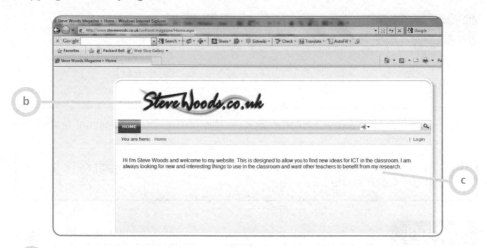

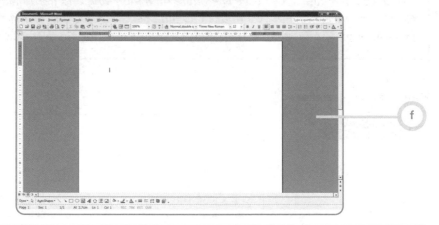

a. Open the programs you want to copy from and to. For this example I have opened Internet Explorer and Microsoft Word.

b. Open a web page.

c. Select/highlight the text you want to copy.

d. Press Ctrl+C to copy (this copies to the Clipboard, but it will seem as if nothing has happened).

e. Click on the Taskbar to switch to Word.

f. The Word document will come to the front.

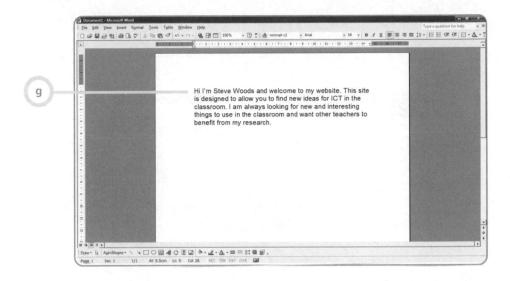

g.

Hi I'm Steve Woods and welcome to my website. This site is designed to allow you to find new ideas for ICT in the classroom. I am always looking for new and interesting things to use in the classroom and want other teachers to benefit from my research.

g. Press Ctrl+V to paste. The text can be changed and edited to suit your needs.

TOP TIP!

This technique is not limited to the example shown; nearly all programs allow copy and paste. Once you are familiar with the operation try it with different programs.

Hyperlinks and internet pictures

A **hyperlink** is a link to an internet page. They are simple to create and can save time, but most importantly allow you to keep pace in your lessons. Another benefit of hyperlinking is that you only expose your class to images and text you have vetted. It is not good practice to use a **search engine** in front of your class. Even with safeguarding programs in place, innocent searches can result in inappropriate content and advertising. In this chapter you will learn how to jump directly to the internet page you require from Word, PowerPoint and SmartNotebook. Other programs also allow hyperlinking, but knowing the following will allow you to feel confident in almost any popular application.

Copying a web address for hyperlinking

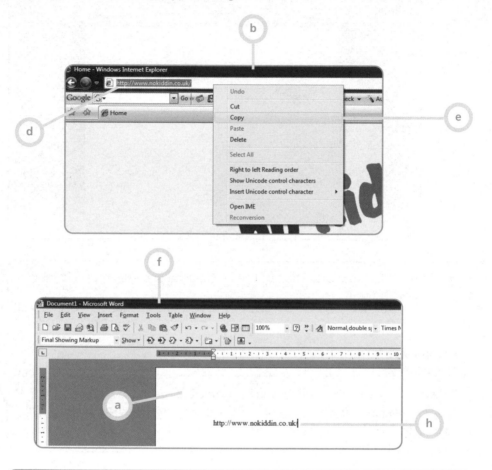

a. Open a new or existing Word document. This example uses a new document.

b. Leave the Word document open and open your internet browser (here it is Internet Explorer). Both programs will be open on your Taskbar.

c. Find the page you want to hyperlink to.

d. Right-click in the Address bar.

e. The address will be highlighted and a menu will appear, select Copy.

f. Use the Taskbar to swap back to your Word document.

g. Click on the page to make sure it is activated.

h. Paste the address in place (using Ctrl+V).

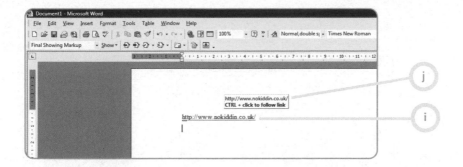

i. Press Enter and the address will change colour and a line will appear below it.

j. Hover the mouse over the hyperlink, press and hold Ctrl and left-click. The internet page will open.

Hyperlinking in PowerPoint

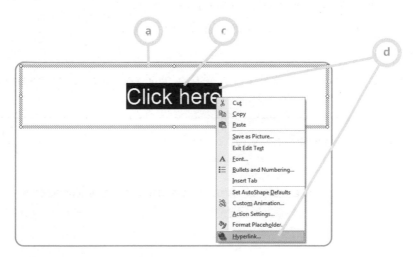

a. Open PowerPoint.

b. Copy the address of the web page you want to hyperlink to by right-clicking in the Address bar and selecting Copy.

c. In PowerPoint add your text or insert ClipArt (this method works for both).

d. Right-click and select Hyperlink from the menu that appears.

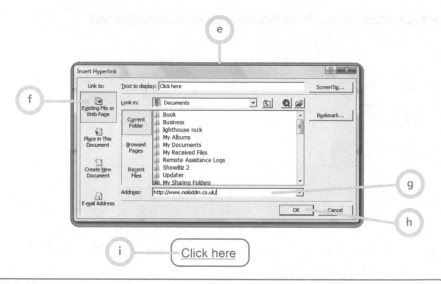

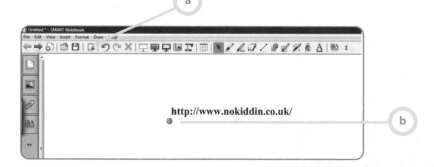

e. The Insert Hyperlink dialog box will appear.

f. Make sure Existing File or Webpage is selected.

g. Click in the Address box and paste (use Ctrl+V).

h. Select OK.

i. Your text or ClipArt will now be a hyperlink. Remember that the show must be running for it to work.

Hyperlinking in SmartNotebook 10

Simple:

a. Copy the web address by right-clicking in the Address bar. Open Smart-Notebook and click on the Paste icon (or use Ctrl+V).

b. The address will appear with a blue globe. Click on the globe to jump to the internet page you chose.

Via an object:

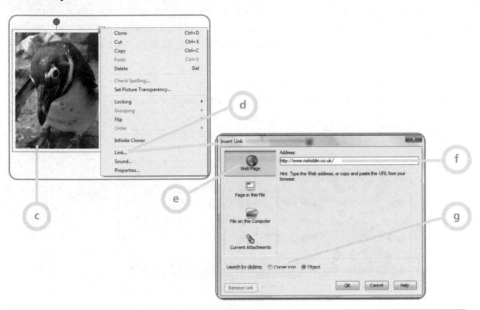

c. Copy the web address by right-clicking in the Address bar. Insert an object (here the penguin).

d. Right-click on the object to open the drop-down menu and select Link.

e. The Insert Link dialog box will open. Select Web Page.

f. Paste the address here.

g. Selecting Corner icon gives a small globe (as in the simple option on page 26); selecting Object makes the picture a link.

Using pictures from the internet

I strongly believe in one rule: never copy and paste from the internet! Always 'Save Picture As'.

The internet can provide some great images to inspire and motivate but you need to take care in collecting them as you could unintentionally send a member of your class to a page you would not deem appropriate.

A really simple way to get an image into your work from the internet is to copy and paste it. The problem is that when you copy an image you can also copy any hyperlinks the picture may have. We all know that internet pages change regularly and the text that accompanied your picture, which was appropriate when you copied the picture, may not be so appropriate when the hyperlink is followed.

In some instances, when a picture that has been copied is changed on a web-site it will also change in the program it has been copied to. You would be surprised at the number of pupils who don't understand why their picture has changed to something completely irrelevant (and sometimes inappropriate as well).

The solution is to save the picture to somewhere you can find it and then insert it where you want it. Or use Screen capture (see Chapter 3).

Saving an internet picture

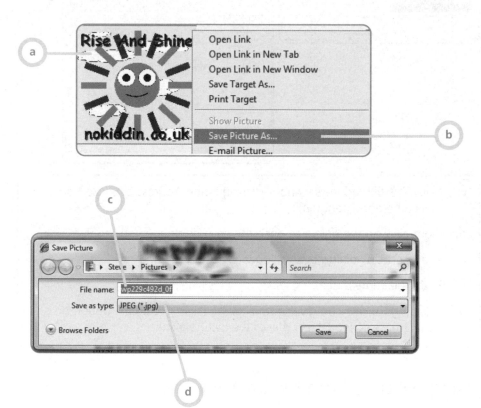

a. Find a picture on the internet that you want to use.

b. Right-click the picture and choose Save Picture As... from the menu.

c. Name the picture and save it where you can find it.

d. Don't worry about changing the file type. If it won't go into the program you want to use then change it to suit (type 'file types' into the help sec-tion of the program to see what it will accept).

TOP TIP!

In most programs you will be able to click on Insert > Picture > From File on the top menu bar to use the picture.

Why not try this?

Practice makes perfect. Why not try an image search for pictures you might need in future lessons and save them where you can find them later (see www.pearsoned.co.uk/essentialguides).

Key ideas summary

The basic skills introduced in this chapter feature in almost every piece of software you currently have and are likely to use in the future. These are the skills that are assumed or only quickly recapped by the modern trainer, but once they are embedded in your daily practice they will make both your day-to-day teaching and any further development in ICT a lot easier.

Building on your foundations – further skills

What this chapter will explore:

- Using Screen capture to get pictures quickly and make them work for you

- Utilising virtual tours and 360-degree panoramas to take your class practically anywhere in the world.

Consolidation is an important part of learning. This chapter builds on the basic skills you acquired in Chapters 1 and 2 and explores two practical tools that can easily be applied across the curriculum with children of all ages.

Screen capture

Screen capture is just like Copy and Paste except you take a copy of the screen (or a section of it) instead of a single object. One benefit of Screen capture is any hyperlinks are not copied (see Chapter 2) because you are taking an image not the actual object. In this chapter we'll explore the most common methods of Screen capture.

Screen capture in SmartNotebook 10

First open SmartNotebook. (It is a good idea to always have SmartNotebook open so you can switch to it quickly using the Taskbar and access the tools available.)

a. Open a website or whatever you want to capture. For this example I have used the banner on my website.

b. Click on the camera icon to open the Capture toolbar . Once you switch the tool on you will capture whatever you draw around on the next click.

c. These buttons capture the whole screen.

d. The Capture toolbar will always be at the front.

e. This button allows a rectangular capture.

f. This button allows you to draw a shape.

After a little practice the capture tool becomes second nature.

Why not try this?

Internet text can be small and difficult for the whole class to see. Use the capture tool to enlarge text. Perhaps even use the highlighter for emphasis (see www.pearsoned.co.uk/essentialguides).

If you have an interactive whiteboard that does not have a Screen capture feature there is a way to capture the screen. Although a little more work is needed, this method can be quite effective with practice. The next figure demonstrates capturing to a Word document, but it is possible to use any application that allows you to paste.

TOP TIP!

Don't panic! Print Screen does not print the screen, it merely copies an image of the whole visible screen to the Clipboard.

Screen capture using Print Screen and Paste

a. Make sure that whatever you want to capture is on the screen.

b. On the keyboard there is a button with 'PrtSc' (or Print Screen) written on it. Hold down Ctrl and press PrtSc. The screen will now be copied to the Clipboard. Nothing will appear to happen – you have just taken a picture of what you are looking at. (Sometimes, if you are using a laptop, the Fn (function) button is used instead of Ctrl. The best way to find out is trial and error.)

c. Go to the document you want to paste to and paste the image. I have used a Word document here.

d. In Microsoft Office documents you can crop the image using the Picture toolbar (if you can't see the toolbar go to View > Toolbars > Picture).

e. The Picture toolbar.

f. This is the Crop tool. Click on it to crop the image.

g. Drag the handles around the image to crop it.

Why not try this?

Pause a movie and capture stills to make a story board to help your class recap or make notes once you have watched it (see www.pearsoned.co.uk/essentialguides).

Virtual tours

A virtual or panoramic tour is a set of photographs stitched together to give the effect of being able to look around 360 degrees. These tours are becoming increasingly popular and, although they can vary in standard, with a little patience and perseverance you can usually find a tour to make for a more exciting and interactive lesson.

A good example is the virtual tour of Merton College, available at www.chem.ox.ac.uk/oxfordtour/merton. By clicking on different areas on a map you are taken to a 360-degree view of that area. Take a look at this tour first to get an idea of what you will be searching for. You may need to download QuickTime the first time you visit the tour. This is a free download that should start automatically. Otherwise go to www.apple.com/quicktime/download/ and follow the onscreen instructions (there is no need to download iTunes – unless you want it).

Searching

In searching, a lot can depend on the search engine you use and what you type into it. Try typing 'virtual tour' and check your results. Then try 'panoramic tour'. You will find totally different results. Knowing this can speed up your quest for what you want. Use the following as a guide to searching.

If you are just browsing for tours search using the following:

> virtual tour
>
> panoramic tour
>
> panorama
>
> 360 virtual tour
>
> 360 panoramic tour
>
> 360 panorama
>
> virtual tour 360
>
> panoramic tour 360
>
> panorama 360.

All will give slightly different results. For a specific tour search using the following:

> *your topic* virtual tour
>
> *your topic* panoramic tour

and other combinations as above.

Using a virtual tour to make a storyboard

To get more from a virtual tour you can capture stills to make a storyboard. The following steps can be done on any computer with an internet connection and Microsoft Word or Publisher (or any similar program). A good interactive whiteboard will have a shortcut tool for this process.

The following example uses Publisher as it will allow pictures to be saved and used in Photo Story 3 (see Chapter 4) but will work in any program that allows you to paste.

> **Why not try this?**
>
> If you have a Smart software installed you can use the capture tool to do this instead of Print Screen (see www.pearsoned.co.uk/essentialguides).

Capturing a virtual tour to make a storyboard

a. Open a blank publication in Microsoft Publisher.

b. Make sure you are connected to the internet, then open your browser and go to your virtual tour (we are using the virtual tour of Merton College: www.chem.ox.ac.uk/oxfordtour/merton/).

c. Choose an area (any circle where the link finger appears).

d. An interactive panoramic photograph will appear. Left-click and hold to look around within the panorama (this may take some practice).

e. If the panorama does not appear, download QuickTime (see text for information on how to do this).

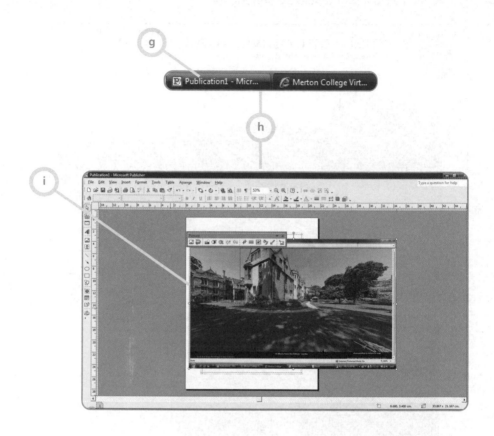

f. When you find the area that you wish to capture, let go of the mouse and press PrtSc/Print Screen (see the figure on Screen capture using Print Screen and Paste).

g. Click on the blank publication on the Taskbar to swap from the internet to Publisher. Do not close either program.

h. Paste the contents of the Clipboard into Publisher (press Ctrl+V).

i. Click on the picture to get manipulation handles, and resize it.

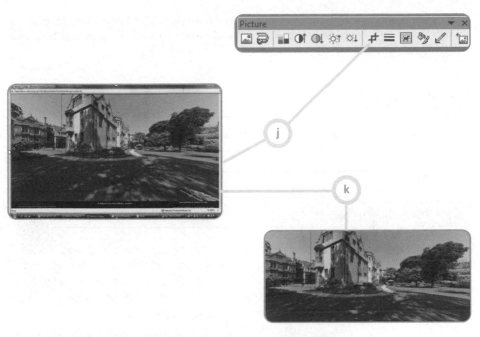

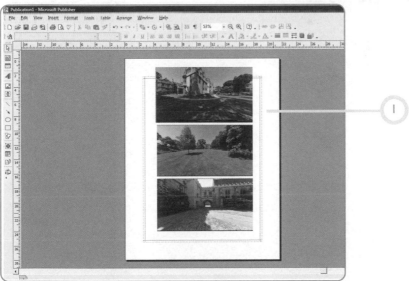

j. To trim the picture, click on the Crop tool on the Picture toolbar (see the figure on Screen capture using Print Screen and Paste).

k. Crop the border to neaten.

l. Repeat the above steps to make a visual storyboard.

With a little practice this method can be used as part of a lesson to make story-boards with your class whilst allowing the children to explore a virtual tour and create their own stories.

Why not try this?

Practise talking whilst you create a virtual storyboard. See a real time demonstration online at www.pearsoned.co.uk/essentialguides.

Key ideas summary

Using a visual stimulus is an easy way to keep your pupils focused. Recapping using images you have captured, in addition to your usual methods, does not depend on the literacy skills of your class and appeals to the more visual learners. Some interactive whiteboards will even allow you, or your pupils, to annotate the images. Why not give it a try?

Part 2

Tools for the modern classroom

Introduction

In the past it was difficult to incorporate media such as music and film into our everyday teaching. Today you can almost guarantee that, at any given time during the day in your school, at least one teacher will be delivering a lesson from PowerPoint or a website. Modern children need more! How many 'PowerPoint style' presentations has a child seen by the time they reach Year 6? How many children have already seen the website that is being shown? I am not saying that using PowerPoint is a bad idea, but adding the 'wow!' factor to lessons is becoming increasingly more difficult.

It used to be true that amazing, fancy presentations came from expensive and time-consuming software. Today, freeware and open-source software has changed everything. Chapters 4–7 will explore the following:

- **Photo Story 3** – instant, effective presentations.
- **Picasa 3** – organise, edit and share your pictures.
- **Scratch** – control and modelling made easy.
- **Audacity®** – audio recording and editing.

Whether exploring a virtual tour to enhance story writing or simply collecting evidence that would otherwise be lost, these four free programs provide you and your pupils with a fun and exciting experience, and something that, once mastered, you will be lost without.

Photo Story 3

What this chapter will explore:

- Using the Wizard to help you make a presentation
- Editing pictures and adding text and titles
- Creating music to accompany your project
- Saving and playback

Photo Story 3 is an easy way to make pictures on your computer come alive. A **Wizard** (a step-by-step guide) takes you through making your presentation. It helps you edit your pictures, add text, narrate, and create or import background music. You then choose the format you want to play your presentation in and, at the click of a button, are ready to show the world … or your class. The Wizard is so simple to use even young children can use it and achieve a professional looking presentation with little or no support.

Before you start you need to download and install Photo Story 3. This is a free download and can be found through a search engine or at www.microsoft.com/windowsxp/using/digitalphotography/photostory/default.mspx.

Making a photo story

a. Open Photo Story 3, choose Begin a new story and click Next.

b. You need to have pictures on your computer, which can be either digital photographs or pictures you have saved from the internet (for saving pictures from the internet see Chapter 2).

TOP TIP!

An internet image search can yield lots of images very quickly. Make a folder and point your class towards it, which not only keeps them safe from the internet but also narrows their choice, and therefore reduces the time wasted on deciding which image to use.

Importing and editing pictures

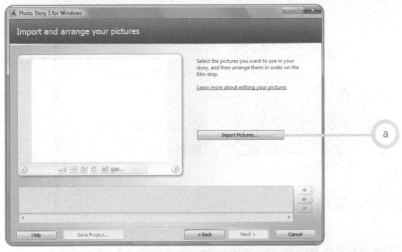

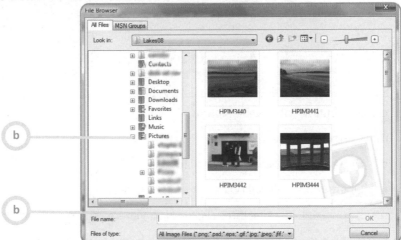

(a.) Click Import Pictures.

(b.) Find the pictures you want to import, and click OK.

TOP TIP!

Click here and drag to select more than one picture. You will draw a rectangle and see the images change as they are selected. You can also hold down Ctrl to select individual pictures from a group.

c. This button rotates the picture.

d. Corrects red eye in the picture.

e. Corrects colour levels in the picture.

f. Opens more edit options.

g. If you want more pictures click Import Pictures again and repeat step (b).

h. If any pictures have black borders click here to auto crop all pictures and remove the borders.

i. Click here to change the current picture.

j. Delete the current picture.

k. You can save your project at any time with this button.

Adding text and a title

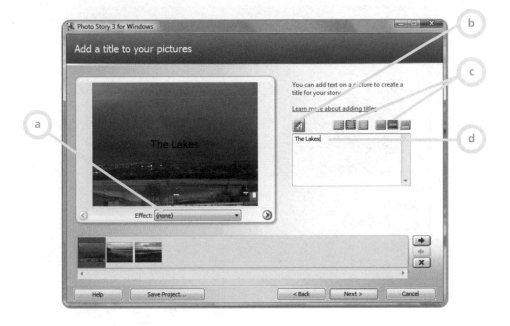

a. Click this button for a drop-down menu of effects you can apply to the picture.

b. Change font colour, size, etc.

c. Change text alignment.

d. Type your text here.

Narration

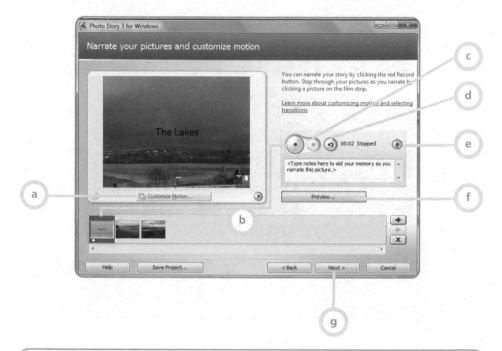

a. This button sets how the picture moves and how long it shows for. Also allows you to change the slide transition.

b. Click here to record narration on the highlighted picture.

c. Stop recording.

d. Undo recording.

e. The first time you use Photo Story 3 click this button and follow the Wizard to set up your microphone.

f. Select the thumbnail you want to start on and click Preview to see the project so far.

g. When you have finished adding narration, click Next to continue.

Why not try this?

Add the same picture a number of times and use the Custom Motion option to make your narration more focused and interesting.

Creating music

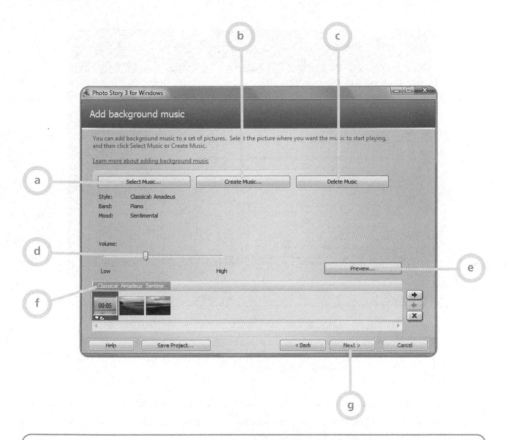

a. Click here to select from the music you have on your system.

b. Allows you to make your own music using a built-in Wizard.

c. Delete music.

d. Change the level of the background music.

e. Preview your project.

f. Music shows above thumbnails when inserted.

g. When you have finished adding music, click Next to continue.

Saving and playback

a. This is the setting to use for full-screen playback to the whole class. Other settings are self-explanatory.

b. Click Browse to select where to save the file.

c. Click Settings to change the quality of your project.

d. You may want to save the finished project in case you want to change anything later.

e. When you are ready, click Next to create the project. This may take a while, depending on the number of pictures and the amount of narration.

When you finish a project there are a number of different export options. If you are uploading to a website, learning platform or any internet-based storage you should try to keep the file size as small as possible so it will download quickly when viewing it. The Send Story in an Email option will give a more manageable file size in this situation.

Why not try this?

Try making a photo story using screen captures from a virtual tour (see www.pearsoned.co.uk/essentialguides for an example.

Key ideas summary

By teaching this application to your class as well as using It yourself you will not only be engaging the children in an interesting activity, but are also modelling the skills you are expecting them to use in a way that they will understand and emulate.

Chapter 5

Picasa 3

What this chapter will explore:

- The tools and functions of Picasa 3 at a glance to save time getting to know this application
- Ideas for using the tools in the classroom environment

Picasa 3 is a free download from Google. It is designed to help you manage, edit and present your photographs quickly and easily. As photographic evidence is becoming increasingly important, due to the more creative approaches we are taking towards teaching and learning, Picasa 3 offers a powerful solution to the needs of the modern teacher. The following figures are a quick reference guide designed to help you get started with the basics. Detailed manuals and tutorials are available through the Help function within Picasa 3.

Quick reference guide

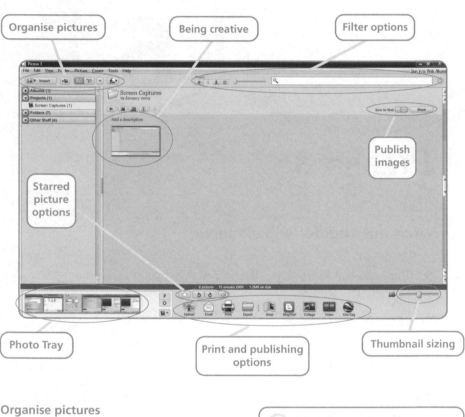

Organise pictures

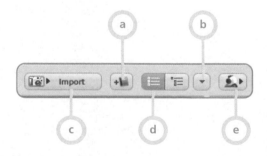

a. Make new album.

b. Sort pictures.

c. Import from camera or other device.

d. Change file view.

e. Take a picture with a webcam (if connected).

These tools allow you to organise your pictures. Plug your camera into the USB port. Switch it on then click Import – Picasa 3 will do the rest.

TOP TIP!

Try handing over management of pictures to your class in the same way that you have monitors for books, etc.

Being creative

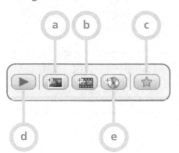

a. Make a collage.

b. Make a picture video.

c. Select starred photos.

d. Play album as slide show.

e. Make a gift CD.

These tools allow you to get creative. In one click you can view a slide show, make a collage for display or even create a video presentation for an assembly.

Filter options

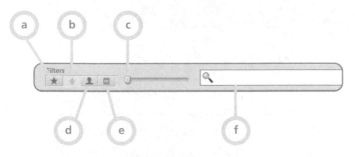

a. Show starred photos.	d. Show photos with faces in.
b. Show uploaded photos.	e. Show videos.
c. Filter by age.	f. Search by keyword.

These tools help you find your photographs by giving you filter options. (See page 58 for starred picture filter options.)

Publish images

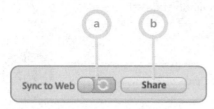

a. Synchronise with your web album.

b. Share pictures online.

These are tools that enable you to publish or share images online. (*Note*: for child protection reasons, it is not recommended that you use these tools with images taken of children in your school.)

Thumbnail sizing

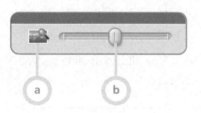

a. Magnify a single picture.

b. Enlarge thumbnails.

Change the size of your thumbnails for easier viewing.

Print and publishing options

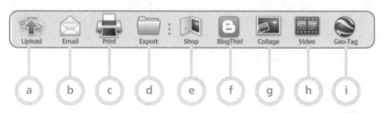

a. Upload to web album.   f. Post pictures on a blog.

b. Email pictures.   g. Create a collage.

c. Print pictures.   h. Make a picture video.

d. Export to new location.   i. Add pictures to Google Earth.

e. Get pictures printed and posted to you.

These tools work in conjunction with the Photo Tray (see below). The Print and Export options will be the tools you use the most, along with Collage and Picture Video. (*Note*: Before using the other tools first check with your school, as even sending images to be printed may breach its child protection policies.

TOP TIP!

Make your displays more attractive by using a digital photo frame. Again, you could get the children to manage the pictures they want to be displayed.

Photo Tray

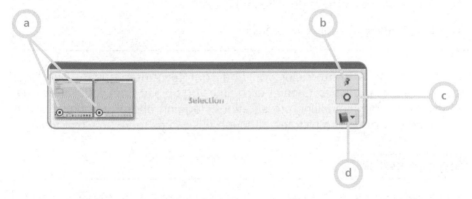

a. Held items have a symbol in the corner.

b. Hold items.

c. Clear tray.

d. Add held items to an album.

The Photo Tray allows you to select images from different folders and present them in different ways using the tools shown above.

Starred picture options

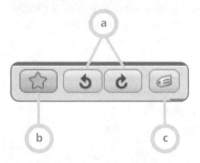

- **a.** Rotate image anti-clockwise and clockwise.
- **b.** Add a star to a picture (for filtering).
- **c.** Tag photos with words for searching.

Adding a star to a photo helps you find your favourites quickly (see Filter options). If you star the best pictures each time you upload from your camera you will save time when compiling presentations. Tagging photos with keywords is also a good way of finding pictures, although this can be more time consuming.

Why not try this?

Take a few photographs, download them to your computer and get a feel for Picasa's editing features (see an example at www.pearsoned.co.uk/essentialguides).

Key ideas summary

Taking photographic evidence is easy. Downloading and sorting hundreds of pictures, because you kept putting it off, is a growing issue for the already stressed teacher. Picasa 3 is a powerful tool that can allow your class to take charge of what they want to show as their best work and also remove some pressure from you.

Chapter

6

Scratch

What this chapter will explore:

- Using Scratch programming software to revitalise current QCA units
- Examples to show how simple it is to adapt Scratch to current teaching

Developed with lifelong learning in mind, Scratch is a free program that helps young people begin to create their own computer-based interactive games, art, stories and music. The Scratch website has great resources, such as movies and printable booklets, to enable you to get started. Due to the extensive support provided by the website I will not dwell on the basics. The figure opposite contains a quick reference guide to refer to whilst you are learning how to use Scratch. Basically, Scratch works by dragging coloured blocks into the script window. Each colour represents a different category motion, such as sensing and control. As Scratch is something you learn through using it, copying the programs in the examples throughout this chapter will enable you to soon get the hang of it. Scratch and all its support material can be downloaded from http://scratch.mit.edu/.

To access help, once downloaded, click on the Want Help? button.

To help you and your class get started I strongly recommend the 'Scratch Cards' found in the support area of the website above or through this direct link:

http://info.scratch.mit.edu/Support/Scratch_Cards.

TOP TIP!

Working through the Scratch Cards is an excellent way to come to grips with Scratch quickly. You could even use them as an introductory exercise for your class.

Quick reference guide for Scratch

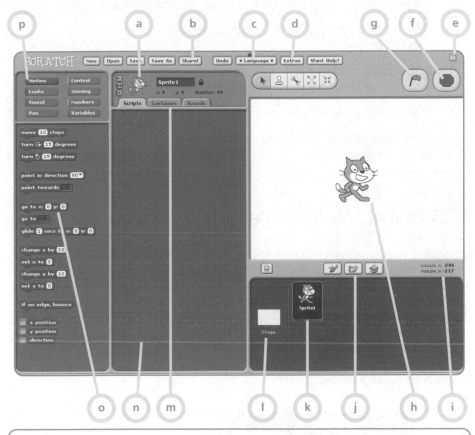

a. Sprite information – tells you about the sprite you are working on.

b. Share project with online community (check school policy before using this).

c. Change language for blocks (might make an interesting MFL lesson).

d. Extras – additional features such as single stepping (slows down script).

e. Project notes – give instructions or simply say who made the project.

f. Stop button.

g. Green flag – starts script running.

h. Sprite – the object that the script acts upon.

i. Mouse coordinates – tells you the position of your mouse cursor.

j. New sprite buttons – draw, open from file or choose a random sprite.

k. Sprite list – all of the sprites you create appear here. When they are highlighted you can edit their script.

l. Stage – the stage also has editable script, sounds and backgrounds.

m. Tabs – click on the tabs to edit sounds, costumes and script for the selected sprites.

n. Script area – drag blocks in and put them together like a jigsaw. The script will apply to the highlighted sprite.

o. Blocks – the commands for the sprite. They fit together like a jigsaw.

p. Click these tabs to change the blocks functions. Each function has a different colour.

QCA Unit 4E: Modelling effects on screen

Modelling effects on screen is one of the units that many teachers dread. Having a whole class creating programs to draw shapes and then crystal flowers is enough to give anyone a headache. Scratch has made this process a lot simpler. Due to the jigsaw piece layout a teacher can see at a glance what stage the children are at and any mistakes they have made. The following diagrams assume you have prior knowledge of Scratch through following the support materials available from the website.

Program to create a square

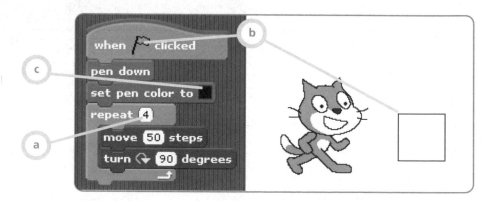

a. Change this number to change the size of the square.

b. If you build this program when you click the green flag the sprite will draw a square.

c. Change this to set the colour of the square

The benefit of using Scratch is that you can change any settings without deleting that part of the program. In the figure on page 62 all you need to do to make the square bigger is to make the number in the Move 50 Steps box bigger. The versatility of Scratch is demonstrated best in the next figure.

Drawing crystal flowers with Scratch

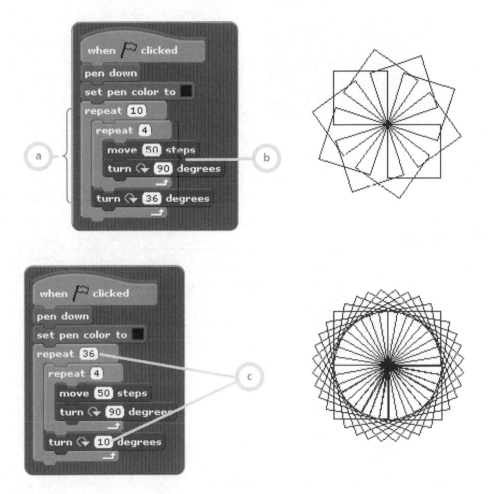

a. This part tells the sprite to repeat the square ten times turning 36 degrees between each instance.

b. This part is the square program (as in the quick reference guide on page 61).

c. Once the program is written changing these numbers (making sure they multiply together to make 360) produces different crystal flower shapes.

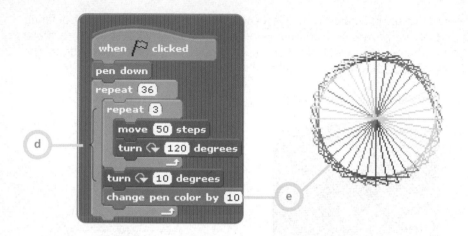

d.   If you want a different shape change the shape program.

e.   Make shapes interesting with a colour effect change.

TOP TIP!

Differentiation in this unit could be through the amount of programming you expect your class to do themselves or the shapes you ask them to create.

Why not try this?

Shape programs do not need to be discarded if you wish to change them. Simply leave them at the side so they can be swapped in and out (see www.pearsoned.co.uk/essentialguides) for an example.

Being able to edit the program means that the children only need to build it once. The learning focus can then move towards investigating more complex shapes and allowing them to see the maths involved more clearly. The sprite also draws the shape quickly; so the child who decides to repeat their shape 360 times and turn it round by 1 degree will not have to sit and do nothing for the rest of the lesson.

Scratch also has built in extensions and incentives. Once you are happy with the children's work they can look at and adapt the preloaded games. Also, because

Scratch is free to download, some members of your class may decide to download it at home and extend the work they have done in school.

Key ideas summary

Scratch is a wonderful introduction to control and has a great deal to offer to other curriculum areas as well. However, although a sensor board can be purchased to allow interaction with light and other real world situations, Sratch is predominantly based in the onscreen 'virtual' world. Writing script to control robots and other gadgets that move and perhaps compete in the real world is an experience that children never forget. For more information and help teaching control technology try contacting your local City Learning Centre to see what they have to offer.

Audacity

What this chapter will explore:

- Making a simple recording with Audacity
- Making a simple project
- Saving into different audio formats

Audacity is another free download that allows you to create audio files, from simple recordings of your voice to professional-sounding multi-track recording and editing. In this chapter you will learn the basics of the program. There is extensive online support and tutorials for Audacity, but please note that it was created for multi-track recording, and therefore the tutorials reflect that. This chapter, therefore, teaches you the tools that you will find most effective for teaching and learning.

Why not try this?

Once you are confident with the skills covered in this chapter try furthering your knowledge with the online tutorials. Audacity can be found through a search engine or at http://audacity.sourceforge.net/.

Recording your voice

To record your voice you need to have a microphone plugged into your computer (some laptops have a built-in mic). Make sure your mic is on and follow the instructions in the following figures.

Recording your voice

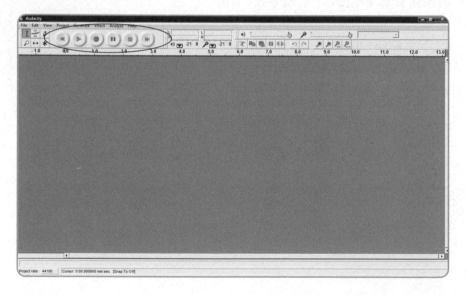

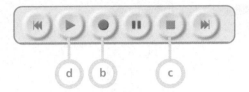

a. Open Audacity and check that your microphone is plugged in.

b. Press Record on the tool bar and talk into the microphone (it can help to write down what you want to say).

c. Press Stop when you have finished recording.

d. Click Play to listen to your recording to check it was captured.

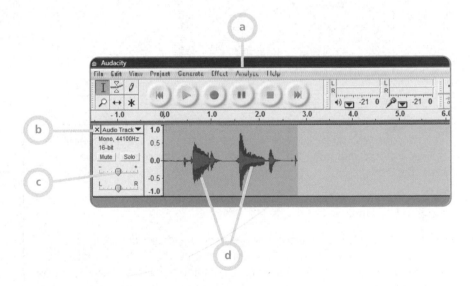

a. The screen will now look something like above. A series of spikes show the recording.

b. Remove recording and start again.

c. Change the volume of the recording.

d. Spikes represent recording.

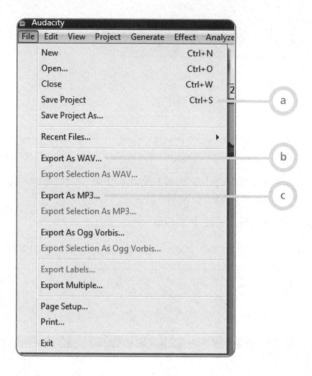

a. To save your recording click File > Save Project. If you want to make the recording compatible with other programs choose one of the export options.

b. Export as WAV (waveform) – this is a format that PCs and most programs recognise.

c. Export as MP3 – this gives a compressed version (smaller file size). Some programs will only accept MP3 files. The first time you do this you need to add the LAME MP3 encoder. Full instructions and a download can be found here: http://audacity.sourceforge.net/help/faq?s=install&item=lame-mp3.

Lots of programs allow you to record your voice, but Audacity allows you to add extra sounds and layer them over one another. The following figures show how you can import additional sounds.

Importing sounds

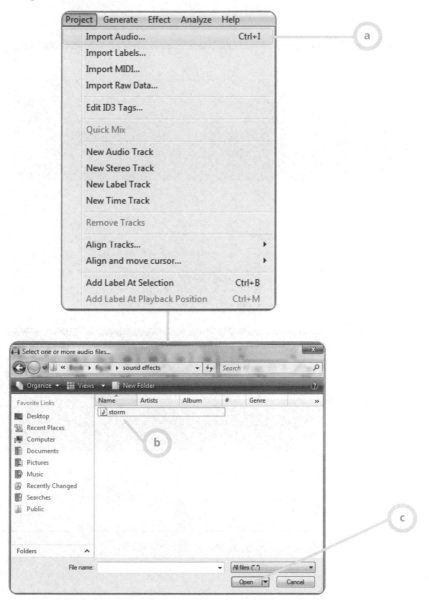

a. Click Project > Import Audio.

b. Find the file you want to import. A storm sound is selected above.

c. Click Open and the sound will insert.

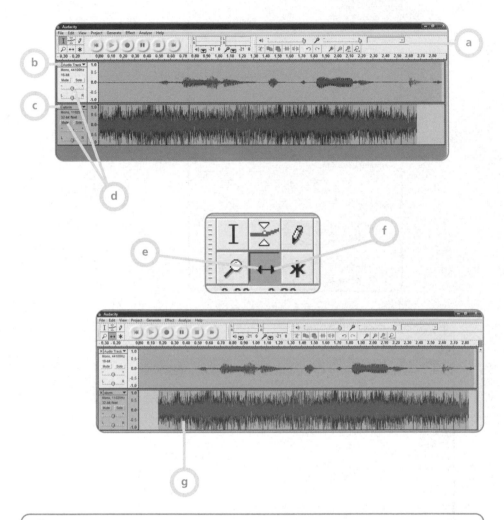

a. The storm sound has been inserted as a new track.

b. Voice recording.

c. Storm sound.

d. Adjust the volume if needed. It is usually better to bring a louder track down to match a quieter track, than take a quieter sound up.

e. Use the Time Shift tool to drag your sound to make it fit better in your composition.

f. Click this to switch Time Shift on.

g. Click and drag the sound.

h. Insert as many sounds as you need by repeating the steps shown in the previous figures.

i. When you are happy with your composition save your project then export it (see Recording your voice).

TOP TIP!

It is always a good idea to save the project as an Audacity project as well as exporting to WAV or MP3. Saving as an Audacity project allows you to go back and change anything you are not happy with. For example, the additional background sounds might be too loud and you need to reduce their volume to make the voice recording stand out.

Why not try this?

Create a regular weather report or news review that can be uploaded to your school's virtual learning environment website. See an example at www.pearsoned.co.uk/essentialguides.

Key ideas summary

With child protection being a priority in schools, audio is a fantastic medium for school websites and virtual learning environments. Audacity allows content to be made quickly and the small file sizes, such as MP3, mean that the uploading time is kept to a minimum. This is ideal for keeping your school's web presence fresh and interesting and, best of all, your class will enjoy it.

Part
3

Creative projects

Introduction

The following projects are a guide to embedding the software and skills from the previous chapters in this book. The ideas for Years 1 and 2 focus a little more on the teacher enhancing how they deliver to the children. From Year 3 onwards the focus moves towards allowing the children to take charge of their own learning journey.

Working creatively involves working for a purpose and getting the best out of your class in terms of quality learning they will enjoy and, hopefully, retain. For the teachers that remember topic webs (a dark time for teaching, when every subject needed to link together, no matter how tediously), note that the creative projects presented here rely on being creative with time and delivery across the curriculum, allowing you to create purposeful activities for your class. It is not necessary to join everything together or change your whole curriculum, but try and consider where you can include ICT within lessons you are already teaching. Chapter 8 shows how ICT can enhance the curriculum and bring the previous chapters into a classroom context. It is up to you whether you use all or just parts of the projects.

Chapter

8

Creative projects

What makes a good creative ICT project?

My personal view of being creative with the curriculum is that some subjects naturally overlap and therefore give you the opportunity to allocate more time to them. This can be done in a number of ways, my favourites being the following:

- You are able to join more than one area together, e.g. ICT and Geography, using the combined time to produce an outcome.

- By adapting your timetable you can cover a unit in a week rather than the normal once a week period of time. This helps keep ideas fresh and motivation high, e.g. you have 10 hours to deliver ICT over half a term but decide to use every afternoon in one week to produce the same result.

For any creative project in this chapter, time management and thorough planning are essential not only for the lessons themselves but also for resources. Will the computer suite or laptop trolley be available? Are the cameras charged, or if they run on batteries are there spares? Are there any other events in the school calendar that will take time from your project?

Evaluation is essential to a good project, but please remember that evaluation is for you! The whole idea is to make something better or easier the next time you do it. Short notes on your lesson plan or in your diary are more than enough. You could even tweak the lesson plan whilst everything is still fresh in your mind, asking yourself questions like: How did the children react? How could you pre-empt their actions? What took more/less time than expected? Evaluation is useless unless you are honest with yourself but done properly will prove most useful.

But, really, what is a good project?

Good is a word we discourage our pupils from using but inevitably use ourselves. A good project is something you will be proud of, something the children will enjoy, learn from and remember, and, most of all, something you will do over again. My only advice, if you do not follow all the ideas here, is pick a topic you know you will repeat next year and plan it thoroughly and evaluate it critically, but, most importantly, never underestimate the ability of the children.

Start small, and then, once you have a good understanding of how a project works, try new ideas and enjoy learning alongside your class.

Year 1 creative project based on existing QCA

For this project I have used the theme of 'ourselves', which is a prominent theme through Year 1.

The idea of the creative units is to use and apply the skills learned through QCA ICT units to other curriculum areas. This section concentrates on how Unit 1A could be used and applied.

Unit 1A is basically about representing real and fantasy situations on the screen. The unit does not necessarily need to be completed before the project is undertaken.

Science 1A: Ourselves

This requires children to draw a representation of themselves and label the parts of their body.

Children start with a photograph of themselves and using the shape tools in a drawing package cover the photograph with shapes that are similar to the body parts. In the example below I have used Microsoft Word as it is common in schools.

Drawing a representation

a. Insert a photograph into the document.

b. Use the drawing tools to cover your body in shapes to represent the body parts. (This could provoke discussion on the shape and purpose of body parts.)

c. Group the shapes by holding down the Shift key and left-clicking them all (if you select the photo click it again to de-select).

d. Then right-click any of the shapes and choose Grouping > Group from the menu that appears.

e. Remove the photograph by left-clicking it and pressing Delete on the keyboard or Cut in the Edit menu and resize the grouped shapes to fit the page. When you resize hold down Shift to keep the proportions the same.

You are left with a representation of the child which can be printed and used for annotation, or coloured and labelled by the more able before printing.

(*Note*: You must save at this stage if you intend to follow the rest of the project – see Chapter 2 on saving and finding work.)

Art 1A: Self-portrait

Use the self-representation to lead into this unit.

Children always struggle with proportion. By using their model, either clipped to the back of a piece of paper as an image to trace or simply as a template, the children will be given the opportunity to be more accurate and produce a better result.

DT 1A: Moving pictures

The children should use computer-generated images or digital photographs of themselves to create a moving picture.

Children are usually given a choice of two or three different levers they can use, then asked to draw their own pictures. They generally find the background easy but struggle with the moving parts as they are generally smaller. To solve this, depending on the story, allow children to use Art Rage 2 (another free download) to paint a large picture, then save it as an image and shrink it. This will make it look more aesthetically pleasing.

Draw it big and shrink it

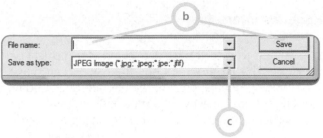

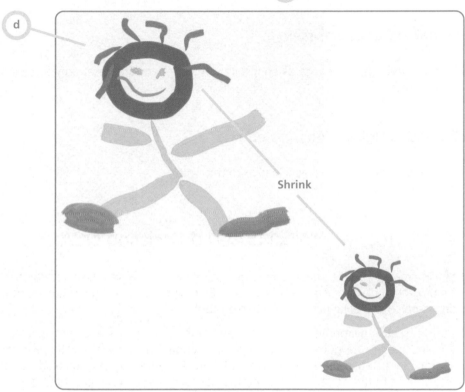

Shrink

a. Child draws picture in Art Rage 2 using the interactive whiteboard. Art Rage 2 (Starter Edition) is free to download and can be found at www.ambientdesign.com/.

b. Click File > Export as Image, name it and then save it where you can find it (see Chapter 2 on saving and finding work).

c. Select JPEG Image from the drop-down menu if not already selected.

d. Insert the image into a document (Word has been used here) and then shrink it using the resize handles. Notice how the picture looks better when reduced and how it does not depend on a good control over fine motor skills. The picture can now be cut out and used as the moving part of the picture.

Music Unit 2: Sounds interesting

Use the body parts theme to record different sounds for musical performance. Children should explore the different sounds their body can make: clapping, stamping, singing, snapping fingers, etc. This can be arranged and rehearsed for a whole class recording (using Audacity) to a previously known song or poem, or one written by the teacher or the children themselves in literacy class.

PE Unit 2: Dance activities

Use the musical performance as an inspiration for a dance representing ourselves and moods.

Citizenship Unit 03: Animals and Us

Use the topic of 'ourselves' as a lead in to this unit.

Year 2 creative project based on existing QCA

For this creative project I have used a geography focus to link the units together. This project combines Picasa 3 and Google Earth, providing a powerful presentation, research and evidence/record-keeping tool.

Relating to our environment and using geographical language and terms, with a clear and interesting purpose, is difficult to accomplish, especially with younger children. By using a medium that is not only extremely visual but also easily accessible at home or using local community facilities, parents can be involved and encouraged to participate in extending this project beyond the classroom. Although I have made links to a number of QCA units, the ideas here could be adapted to suit almost any project.

Geography Unit 5: Where in the world is Barnaby Bear?

This unit or an adaptation of it is probably already running in your school. You will probably already have a number of pictures of the bear in the places he has already visited. For this project the pictures need to be stored on your computer. If they are not yet in a digital format you can easily scan them to make them so.

Tagging into Google Earth

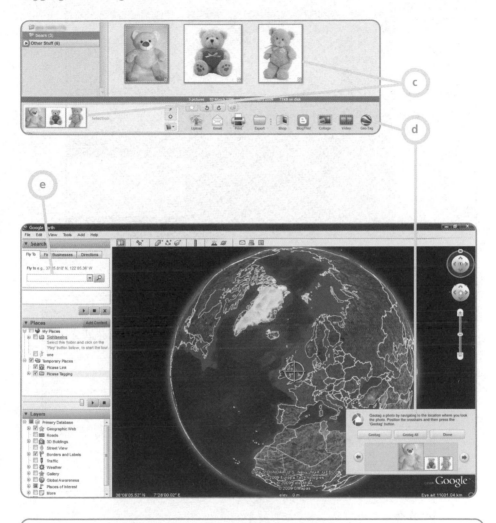

a. For this project you will need: Google Earth (free download), Picasa 3 (see Chapter 5) and the photographs on your computer.

b. Open Picasa 3 and find your bears (it is helpful to save them all into one folder).

c. Select your bears. They will appear in the photo tray.

d. Click on Geotag. Google Earth will open and a Picasa 3 Geotag dialog box will appear in the bottom right corner.

e. Type the place you want to tag a picture to here.

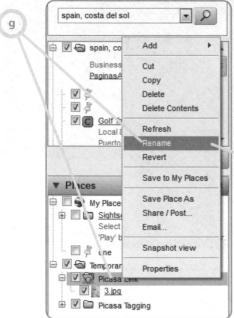

f. Google Earth will zoom into your destination. The picture will be tagged at the point where the target is pointing.

g. Right-click on the Places link folder and click Rename to change it to something you will be able to find again.

h. Click Geotag when you want to insert the picture. It will appear in your My Places window.

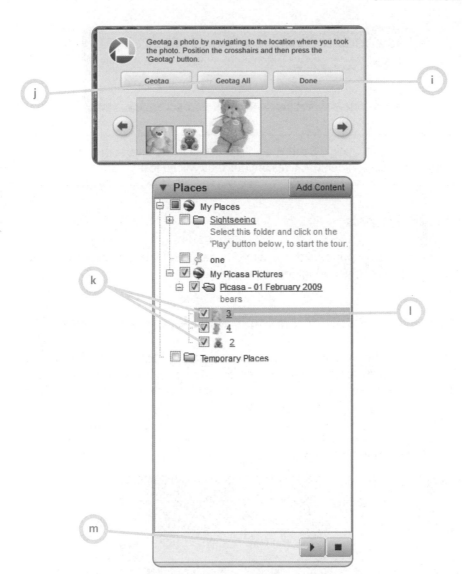

i. Repeat the previous steps to Geotag the rest of the photographs. When you are finished click Done.

j. *Note*: Geotag All puts all of the pictures in one targeted place.

k. Right-click and rename the pictures (using the child's or bear's name may be helpful).

l. Double-click the pictures to be taken to the tagged place.

m. Click the Play button to be flown around the world to see the tagged pictures.

n.

n. When you exit Google Earth you will be asked if you would like to save to your My Places folder. Click Yes or your tags will be lost.

DT Unit 2B: Puppets

For this unit introduce puppets of the world by tagging pictures to their countries of origin using Geotags (see Tagging into Gogle Earth)

Science Unit 2B: Plants and animals in the local environment

Children explore the local environment (usually the school playground/ boundaries), and take pictures and make notes of what they found and where they found it. Using Geotag the children's pictures can be added to the Google Earth view of the school grounds and tagged to the location they were found, as in the figure below:

Science project tagging findings

Expand the project by sending the cameras home and asking the children to take pictures in their gardens or when on trips with their parents.

Tagging on a larger scale

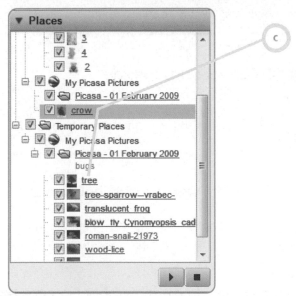

a. Insert the children's pictures using Geotag.

b. Click on the cluster around the school to expand it into a star shape.

c. To keep all of the images together, click and drag the new images into your project folder.

> **d.** Click on the picture name to enlarge it.
>
> **e.** Remember to save any changes when you close Google Earth.

Art Unit 2C: Can buildings speak?

Tag pictures as in the figure on Science project tagging findings. This method of tagging could be used in many different and imaginative ways, for example, school trips.

History Unit 3: What were seaside holidays like in the past?

Tag images in two folders called 'Then' and 'Now' and use them as an introduction and for adding images as you progress through the unit.

History Unit 4: Why do we remember Florence Nightingale?

Combine this unit with ICT Unit 2C: Finding information. Children are expected to find information on a CD-ROM or the internet. Although searching for information on a CD is safer than letting children loose on the internet, not many modern schools use CD-ROMs due to the massive development in the internet since QCA was written. Allowing children to search on the internet could potentially expose them to inappropriate material and, besides the obvious risks, does not always produce results that can be used afterwards. Using screen capture and saving as an image allows you to place content on Google Earth (in this case information on Florence Nightingale) at a geographically correct point, and in a language your class can understand and, more importantly, use for a purpose.

This method builds on the prior knowledge that you can tag an image into Google Earth with Picasa 3 and that by using screen capture you can make anything on your screen an image. Therefore, you can screen capture a worksheet and tag it as easily as you would a photograph.

Tagging information

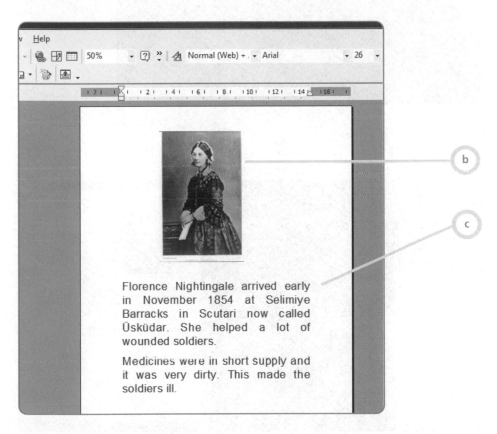

a. Create an information sheet in Word or a similar application then use Screen capture and Save As Picture (see Chapter 3) to make a JPEG image.

b. Insert picture if needed.

c. Use a large font.

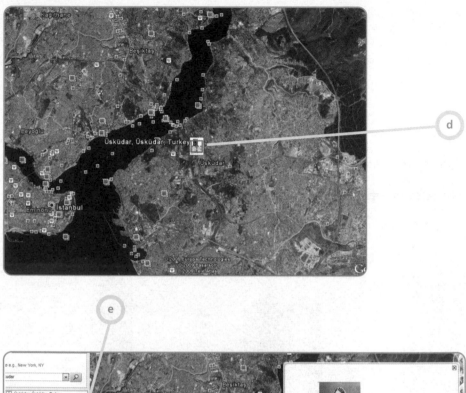

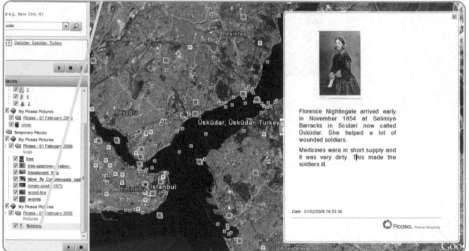

d. Tag the image (see Tagging into Google Earth).

e. Click on the picture name in the Places window to see the information.

f. Repeat these steps to tag as much information as you require.

Year 3 creative project based on existing QCA

For this project I have used a number of smaller focuses which could all be combined but could also stand alone with any topic throughout the year. The topics I have chosen are to help me explain as clearly as possible without getting too bogged down in technical detail.

Music Unit 9: Animal magic

(Also covers ICT 3b: Manipulating sound.)

Before describing this unit I would first of all like to say I can play an instrument and believe that I have delivered some good music lessons over the years. I will also be the first to admit that I have delivered some dreadful ones too! Teaching 30-plus children is not the greatest environment to hone the next chart-topping act, but I strongly believe that music is a very personal art form and that only by making their own music can children truly understand and use the concepts and language expected of them in the QCA units.

This unit asks you to make music to suit an animal's movement for performance. Those who progress further are expected to develop 'several layers of sound'. First, I will choose some animals to describe in music. The following website has some clips with background music that may open up discussion: www.bbc.co.uk/nature/animals/planetearth/realmedia/.

For my example I have chosen penguins. My whole class will be making penguin compositions. Thus, everyone can share ideas and evaluate one another. It also provides a great display opportunity as a penguin makes a great writing frame (just write in the white stomach).

 A Penguin writing frame is available on the website accompanying the book at www.pearsoned.co.uk/essentialguides.

As the class watch the clips encourage the children to use the key words that tie into the music vocabulary for the unit:

- duration – e.g. pulse, rhythm, longer, shorter, sustained;
- tempo – e.g. faster, slower;
- pitch – e.g. steps, jumps/leaps.

The children are expected to use both tuned and untuned instruments. The easiest way to do this would be to visit your local City Learning Centre, or one of the High Schools you feed into, that has audio recording facilities (you will also receive help if you take this route). If this seems a little too extravagant, the same result can be achieved in school. Below I have used a tambourine and a glocken-spiel, as it is almost guaranteed that you will have these in your school. Keyboards would be excellent and increase the range of sounds available.

Building on prior units, children write a rhythmical sentence to describe the movement of their animal. The syllables of the sentence will become the rhythm of the piece of music produced. Encourage the children to make sentences containing eight syllables (8 beats = 2 bars), such as:

penguin sliding from the water

penguin shivering in the cold

penguin hops to the colony

penguin snuggles in with his friends

penguin happy now nice and warm.

As the pace of a song can dictate the mood so can the speed the children read their sentences. It should take 20 to 30 seconds to read the above to create a composition with a sensible pace. If you want a longer composition just double up the sentences or write more.

A discussion of the effect could take place here as the children have a real reference (i.e. their work) to discuss. An attempt to scribe the music using symbols could also be made.

After practising, the children use Audacity to record their sentences, putting emphasis on the syllables.

In the figure below I have spoken my first sentence and then overlaid text to show where the words are.

How the sentence fits into Audacity

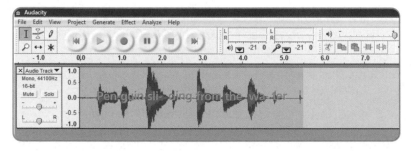

The next step is to take the tambourine and play the rhythm of the syllables. When I press Record I will automatically get a new track – just remember to rewind first.

A movie example of this figure can be seen at www.pearsoned.co.uk/essentialguides.

Adding a rhythm

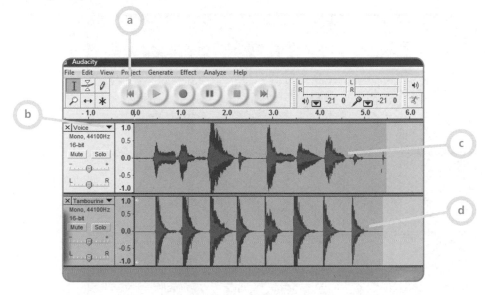

a. Remember to rewind before you record.

b. By clicking on the drop-down menu you can name each track..

c. Voice track.

d. Tambourine track.

TOP TIP!

Always use headphones when recording with a microphone or you will record the previous track as well and may get feedback from the speakers.

Now I can record another layer, playing my repeating pattern. The tambourine track also gives a visual representation of the rhythm: every four spikes is a bar. In the figure below I have this time played my repeating tune on the glockenspiel (using just three notes that sounded nice together) starting on beat 2 of each bar. I have also overlaid the beats to help you visualise them.

A movie example of this figure can be seen at www.pearsoned.co.uk/essentialguides.

Adding glockenspiel

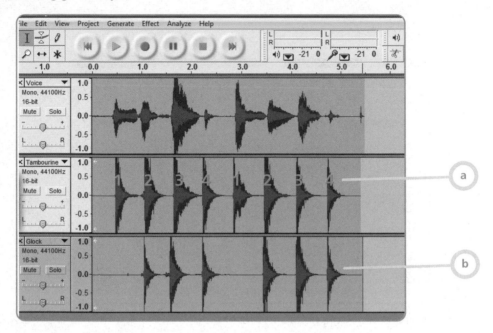

a. Tambourine track with beats labelled.

b. Glockenspiel with three notes repeated on the beat.

Finally, we need to mix the composition. Adjust the volumes and pan settings on each track to taste. Make sure you save the project as well as exporting the final track as we will be using this composition later.

A movie example of this figure can be seen at www.pearsoned.co.uk/essentialguides.

Making a presentation

ICT Unit 3D: Exploring simulations

This can also enhance ICT. When predicting the weather meteorologists use computer simulations to help them. Using the UK weather forecast from the Met Office (www.metoffice.gov.uk/), you can give children the chance to make predictions based on local knowledge, patterns and known facts. You could make a daily event of looking at the satellite picture, making predictions (you could even draw on the interactive whiteboard where clouds or rain will be expected) and then checking them the following day. This may also be an opportunity to improve the children's geographical knowledge of the UK, and their speaking and listening skills.

Geography Unit 7: Weather around the world

Part of this unit looks at specific places and what you would do there. You could spend some time looking at the climate of the natural habitat for your chosen animal using the Met Office website. This could also be combined with Science Unit 3B: Plants and growing, looking again at the 'real-time' weather in their natural habitat.

The idea for this revolves around consolidating prior knowledge, so you may want to use this as an assessment or presentation in an assembly or to parents. This could be done in programs such as PowerPoint or Photo Story 3. I am going to use Photo Story 3 as it is freely accessible and also a lot simpler to use. The basic idea is that the children will make a presentation in the style of a documentary on the chosen animal. The musical composition they made earlier will be used as the background music and the narration will feature the recommended vocabulary and show what the children have learned through this unit.

First you need to have recorded your background music (done with Audacity in the previous section). You could also use the built-in music if you have not chosen to follow the whole project or some children were absent. Re-open your Audacity file and delete the voice track. This will leave you with your background music. Click File > Save As and rename the file so you do not lose the original with the voice.

Next, check the track sounds how you want it to then export it as a WAV or MP3, as shown in the figure overleaf.

Remember to save the exported file where you can find it. It might be wise to make a folder on a shared drive for all of the children to save into.

Next, recording anything, the children will need to compile a storyboard for their ideas. If you allow six pictures and 5 seconds per picture you will have 30 seconds per child. This does not sound like a long time, but careful scripting will allow a lot of information to be packed into that time. We must also consider our audience ... a 15-minute assembly watching 30 penguin presentations may not make you the most popular teacher in the staff room!

Exporting from Audacity

a. WAV (larger file size).

b. MP3 (smaller file size). This takes up less space but you may be asked for a LAME MP3 encoder. If you do not know how to do this don't worry, just save it as a WAV.

Next, the children create a Photo Story 3 file using the six pictures they planned into their script. I am going to assume that you can already insert pictures and narrate. If unsure about what to do please refer to Chapter 4. It is always a good idea for the first slide to contain the child's name as a title.

Once the pictures are narrated and transitions, custom animation, etc. are set you will reach the Add background music section.

Adding Music to Photo Story 3

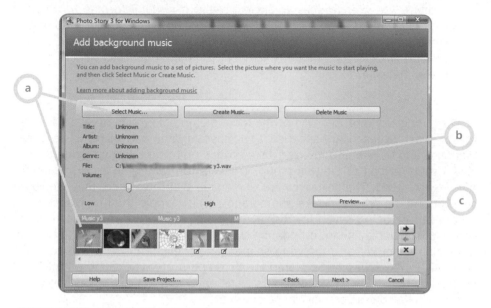

a. Click Select Music and add the composition. It appears at the bottom of the dialog box.

b. Change the music volume to suit.

c. Click Preview to test the story.

The final step is to export as a movie, again saving the files where they can be found (a new 'finished project' folder may be appropriate).

All you need to do now is make sure that they all play in Media Player before you hold your assembly. It is always best to test anything before you show it, even if you only check the facts the children have used and their spelling.

Year 4 creative project based on existing QCA (I)

This project revolves around Art Unit 4A: Viewpoints. This unit focuses on encouraging the children to research their own work and become inspired by an idea, in this case dream sequences, then go on to develop printing blocks and a final piece. According to QCA, those who progress further will:

'Explore a range of ideas using shape, tone and texture seen in the built environment; use sketchbooks and select relevant visual information for their work; experiment with photographic and printing techniques to inform and extend their ideas; compare the ideas, methods and approaches used in their own and others' work; modify their work to reflect their own view of its purpose and meaning.'

(QCA 2000, Art Unit 4a: Viewpoints)

It was during this unit that one of the more memorable moments that changed my approach to teaching happened. I had spent a large part of my Easter break planning and developing my own take on this unit and I was very proud of it. First, I sold the idea to the year group. We were to produce an art exhibition for parents to attend. The children were to manage their own time, they would be sent around the school to take photographs, which would then be cropped and edited before being saved for display on a digital photo frame placed in the centre of the display board outside the classroom. I encouraged them to bring in magazine clippings of interesting shapes, and their homework was to make sketches in the styles we explored in our preparatory weeks. I thought I had cracked it. The children's sketch books were amazing and I can honestly say that every child had produced work to be proud of.

(I should explain at this point that I am a strong believer in using the language and vocabulary of a subject in context, which can sometimes be overlooked in the need to provide physical evidence of children's work in the limited time available. So I always encourage children to use our 'artistic words' in art and our 'historical words' in history, etc. The children try their best to use them correctly, as there are prizes involved and I always make a big fuss.)

So it was when I was asking a child with a fantastic sketch book of ideas what inspired him to take such unusual angles for pictures, and why he had chosen a section of a wall to make a printing block, that my whole big fancy 'look-at-me' project came crashing down. The child, who shall remain anonymous, said

'Because you told me to sir.'

He did not understand that the research was to inspire and give their art work purpose and meaning. He had simply gone through the motions and was doing what he was told. As I investigated further, more and more children did not understand the real reason for doing all of this preparatory work. I could have just given them some stimuli, explained and said 'go'.

Although the exhibition happened, and parents came to see the big event their children had been working towards, the words of the one honest child stuck with me. When I evaluated I promised myself that next time I would give that unit real purpose, and the following is how I approached it.

First, I had to create a real purpose, which would be relevant to the children. To do this I took the dream sequence idea but, to focus the taking photographs and sketching, I started through literacy. The children wrote poetry around the topic of dreams. This poem, when combined with music, ICT and art topics, will help the children to make choices that they can later explain (in subject-specific vocabulary) to achieve the outcome expected of 'a child who progresses further' (quoted from the QCA expectations).

My revised project asked the children to develop a Photo Story 3 presentation (this could also easily be done with PowerPoint or a short film) to explain the reason for their choices in their art work. Now, because the children's decisions will be based on creating a piece of art to visually represent something that is already real to them, when asked 'Why did you choose that?' not only will the child find it easier to answer, but the teacher can then challenge the child and set targets to stretch them because there is something both teacher and child can relate to. Therefore, questioning can move from 'Why have you chosen that angle?, to 'How does that angle enhance your poem?'

Year 4 creative project based on existing QCA (II)

Literacy Year 4 Poetry Unit 1: Creating images

This unit is a perfect opportunity to use literacy across the curriculum. The children write a poem that uses the imagery to be used throughout the project.

Music Unit 13: Painting with sound

(This also can cover some of the objectives in ICT Unit 3B: Manipulating sound if in a split year group.)

Using Audacity the children create a 'soundscape' that paints a musical picture for the background of their poem. Again, throughout teaching, giving the children opportunities to use subject-specific vocabulary to describe their creations is essential and allows you to quickly identify their level of understanding.

First, you will need to find some royalty-free sound effects on the internet and download them to a folder where you and the children will be able to find them. A simple web search for 'royalty-free sound effects' will give a number of potential sites. Personally, I would not allow the children to search for themselves as too much choice will mean they will never get around to making a composition, and, as noted earlier, it is not wise to allow children to search freely on the internet. I like to use the following website as it tells you how to save the sounds once you get to them: www.partnersinrhyme.com/pir/PIRsfx.shtml.

Free sound effects website

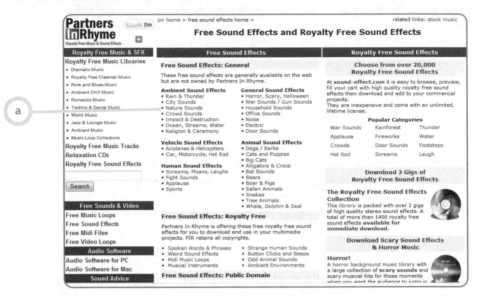

Partners InRhyme twit this	pir home > free sound effects home >	related links: stock music
	Free Sound Effects and Royalty Free Sound Effects	

Royalty Free Music & SFX	Free Sound Effects	Royalty Free Sound Effects

a — Royalty Free Music Libraries
- Dramatic Music
- Royalty Free Classical Music
- Rock and Blues Music
- Ambient Chill Music
- Romantic Music
- Techno & Dance Music
- World Music
- Jazz & Lounge Music
- Ambient Music
- Music Loop Collections

Royalty Free Music Tracks
Relaxation CDs
Royalty Free Sound Effects

[Search]

Free Sounds & Video
Free Music Loops
Free Sound Effects
Free Midi Files
Free Video Loops

Audio Software
Audio Software for PC
Audio Software for Mac

Sound Advice

Free Sound Effects: General

These free sound effects are generally available on the web but are not owned by Partners In Rhyme.

Ambient Sound Effects
- Rain & Thunder
- City Sounds
- Nature Sounds
- Crowd Sounds
- Impact & Destruction
- Ocean, Streams, Water
- Religion & Ceremony

Vehicle Sound Effects
- Airplanes & Helicopters
- Car, Motorcycle, Hot Rod

Human Sound Effects
- Screams, Moans, Laughs
- Fight Sounds
- Applause
- Sports

General Sound Effects
- Horror, Scary, Halloween
- War Sounds / Gun Sounds
- Household Sounds
- Office Sounds
- Noise
- Electric
- Door Sounds

Animal Sound Effects
- Dogs / Barks
- Cats and Puppies
- Big Cats
- Alligators & Crocs
- Bat Sounds
- Bears
- Boar & Pigs
- Safari Animals
- Snakes
- Tree Animals
- Whale, Dolphin & Seal

Free Sound Effects: Royalty Free

Partners In Rhyme is offering these free royalty free sound effects for you to download and use in your multimedia projects. PIR retains all copyrights.

- Spoken Words & Phrases
- Weird Sound Effects
- Midi Music Loops
- Musical Instruments
- Strange Human Sounds
- Button Clicks and Beeps
- Odd Animal Sounds
- Ambient Environments

Free Sound Effects: Public Domain

Choose from over 20,000 Royalty Free Sound Effects

At sound-effect.com it is easy to browse, preview, fill your cart with high quality royalty free sound effects then download and add to your commercial projects.
They are inexpensive and come with an unlimited, lifetime license.

Popular Categories

War Sounds	Rainforest	Thunder
Applause	Fireworks	Water
Crowds	Door Sounds	Footsteps
Hot Rod	Screams	Laugh

Download 2 Gigs of Royalty Free Sound Effects

The Royalty Free Sound Effects Collection
This library is packed with over 2 gigs of high quality stereo sound effects. A total of more than 1400 royalty free sound effects available for immediate download.

Download Scary Sound Effects & Horror Music

Horror!
A horror background music library with a large collection of scary sounds and scary musical hits for those moments when you want the audience to jump in.

NEW! **Amazon Nights** jungle ambience CD — **b**

Ocean Surf	**Wind**
Ocean Surf 1	Wind 1
Beach Surf 1	Windy
Beach Ocean 2	Wind Howl
Beach Surf 3	• **Strong Wind CD** •
Gulls	Wind 2
• **Ocean Surf CD** •	Wind 3
Ocean 1	Wind 4
Ocean 2	Wind 5
Ocean Edge	Wind Sand
Ocean Lap	• **Blustery Wind CD** •
Ocean 3	Storm
Ocean Wave 1	Hurricane
Ocean Gulls	Wind Chimes
Ocean Wave 2	Key Chimes
Ocean 4	
• **Soothing Waters CD** •	**Swamp**
Ocean Wave Big	Swamp 1
Ocean Waves	Swamp 2
Ocean 5	• **Jungle Rain CD** •
Ocean Surf	Swamp 3
Ocean Surf	Swamp 4
Ocean lap	
Ocean Surf	**Jungle**
Ocean Sea	Dark Woods
Ocean Wave	Jungle 1
	Jungle 2
Forest	Jungle 3
Forest	• **Jungle Waterfall CD** •
Forest Night	Jungle 4
• **Stormy Night CD** •	Jungle 5

a. Click on the type of effects you would like. Nature Sounds can give a dreamy effect.

b. Choose your sound effect.

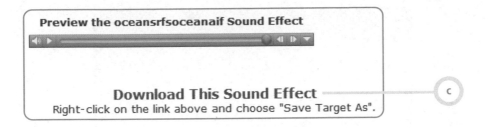

Preview the oceansrfsoceanaif Sound Effect

Download This Sound Effect ———————— c

Right-click on the link above and choose "Save Target As".

---

c. Right-click and choose Save Target As. Remember to save it somewhere children can access as well.

I recommend you download five or six sounds up to a maximum of ten. The more sounds you have the harder it will be for your class to decide which one use, which will waste time.

Using Audacity to create a soundscape

For this the children will use the click track option (a metronome) to set the pace of their project. Open Audacity and start a new project. It is wise to save this project as you go, so click File > Save Project As and save it where it can easily be found. This may be a folder you have set up specifically for the project.

Audacity painting with sound

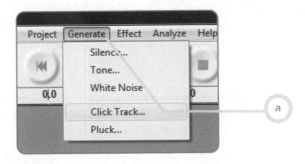

---

a. Click Generate > Click Track.

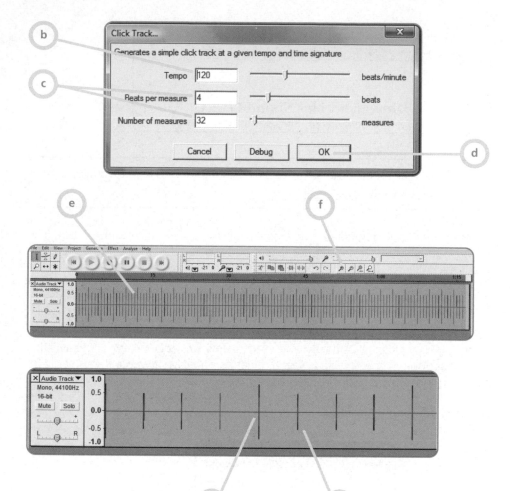

b. Set the tempo to the desired pace. This could be part of a class discussion (too fast makes the poem difficult to read).

c. Don't worry about these settings, keep the default values (i.e. leave them alone!).

d. Click OK to put your track in place.

e. The click track appears as a track in your project. Click Play to hear it.

f. Click on the magnifying glass to zoom in on your project.

g. Zoom in to make the beats easier to see.

h. The higher pitched click represents the first beat in every bar (4 counts).

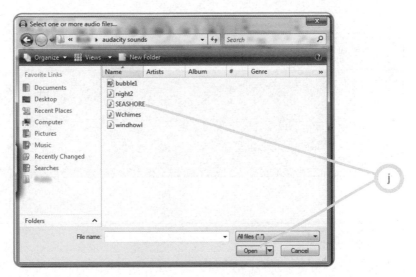

i. Click Project > Import Audio.

j. Find your downloaded sounds, select one and click Open.

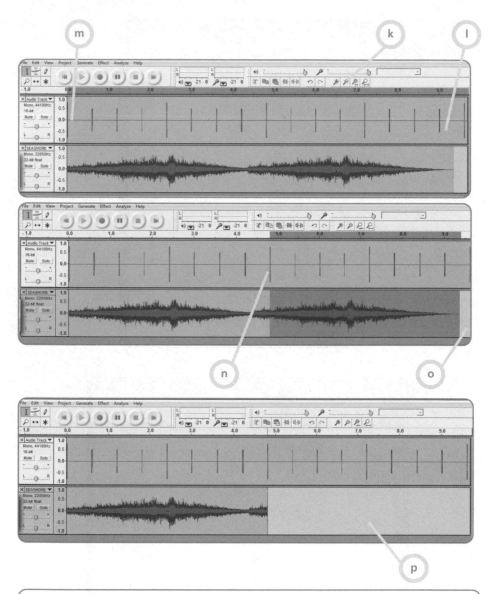

k. Zoom back in.

l. The sound clip lasts for nearly 4 bars. I want a maximum of 2 bars.

m. The first beep is beat 1. Do not count this.

n. End of the 8th beat.

o. Click and drag from here to highlight the sound clip up to the 8th beat.

p. Click Edit > Cut (or use Ctrl+X) to cut the unwanted part of the track.

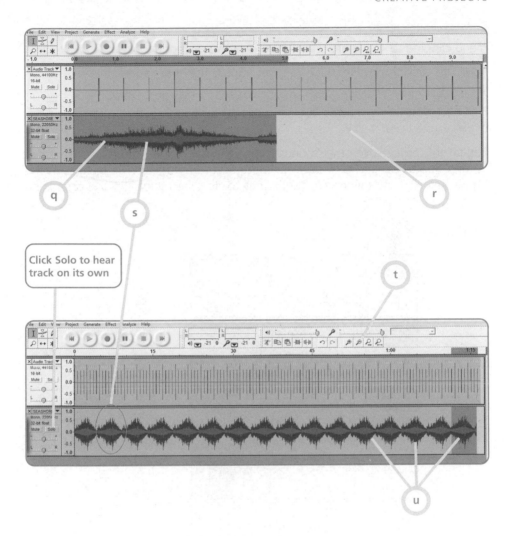

Click Solo to hear track on its own

q. You are left with a sound clip that is exactly 8 beats long.

r. Click and drag to highlight the clip again but this time copy it: use Edit > Copy or Ctrl+C.

s. Same clip zoomed in.

t. Zoom out to see the whole project.

u. Press the right arrow on the keyboard and paste (Ctrl+V) another instance of the sound clip. Repeat until the sound has reached its desired length.

By using the click track the children can clip sounds to fit with the beat. I recommend clipping to 4 or 8 beats as this makes for easy repetition.

Now the click track is in place you can import the first sound that you downloaded from the internet.

Play back your newly pasted track and hear the natural rhythm created by pasting a cropped clip.

Repeat this process for other sounds. When the next sound clip is inserted it can be dragged below the click track for more accurate editing. The pictures in the figure below show this process and what to do when your clip is shorter than 4 beats.

Shorter clips

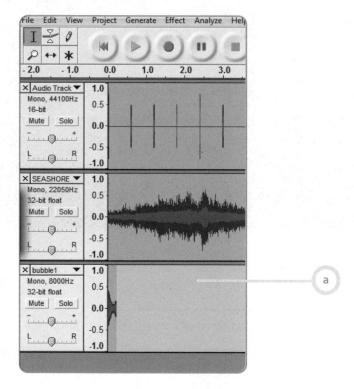

a. Import sound file.

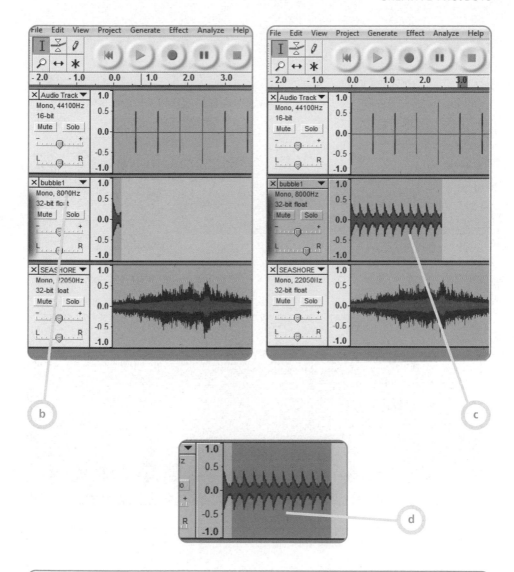

b. Click here and drag the sound file below the click track to make it easier to work with.

c. Copy and paste the sound file to reach the 4th beat.

d. Highlight all of the new instances. Leave the original untouched.

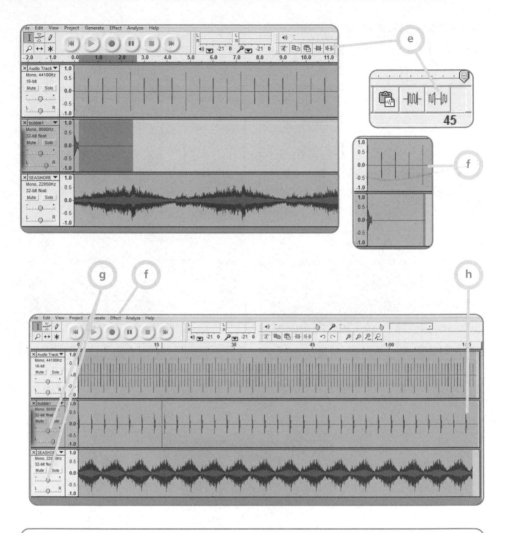

e. Click the Silence Selection button.

f. Cut the clip to exactly 4 beats.

g. Adjust volume and pan to suit.

h. Copy and paste to end of project.

Add more tracks if needed and finally the poem. (Remember that it is essential to use headphones when using a microphone.)

Once the poem is added you may find that the background is too long. By cutting the ends from the background tracks and using fade, a professional end can be achieved, as shown in the next figure.

Fading out

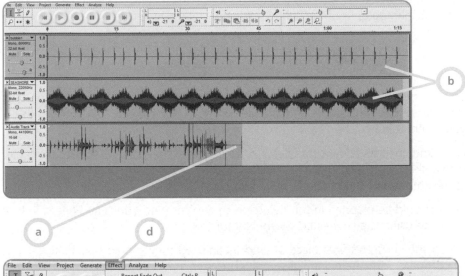

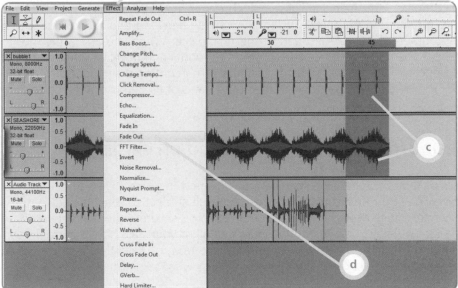

a. The poem is too short for the background.

b. Cut the excess from the background tracks, leaving approx 8 beats after the poem ends.

c. Highlight the section after the poem ends.

d. Click Effects > Fade Out.

Now your background soundscape will fade out after the poem finishes. This can be exported as a WAV or MP3 file and added to a PowerPoint or Photo Story 3 project that uses photographs of the finished art work created in Art Unit 4a: Viewpoints.

Art 4D: Viewpoints

This unit depends only on the poem already being written for inspiration. (As mentioned before, there is no particular order to the projects – it all depends on your timetable.)

Once the children have a stimulus (i.e. their poem) they can go about taking pictures, sketching. etc. (basically, follow the unit but focus on creating a visual representation of their poem).

Time should be planned in for discussion of choices with adults and peers, with a focus on using the suggested vocabulary for the unit.

When the children's final piece of work is finished they should take pictures of it to compare with their original stimuli. This can then be put into Photo Story 3. The original photograph or inspiration can be narrated and then faded into a photograph of the relevant part of the final piece. When you assess the movies there is then a clear link to the children's thoughts and development and plenty of opportunities for them to use vocabulary in a context they understand. Naturally the children will put forward their own views of its purpose and meaning.

Year 5/6 creative project based on existing QCA

Lots of topics in school are imaginary, so I wanted to give my class something real to work with. I find spreadsheets quite a dull subject to teach because in my experience they never become real and, to some children, the numbers seem to change by magic. Can you honestly say that all of your class have a better understanding of spreadsheets when you finish the unit, or have they just learned to copy patterns into boxes? (Try asking your class what spreadsheets actually do.)

So how do you make spreadsheets become real? The answer lies in making a mini business and proving that a spreadsheet lets you manipulate data quickly. As with real life, you need to hold some things back to surprise the children as they run their mini business, which will force them to change their spreadsheets to keep within budget and adapt to new situations.

This creative project was inspired by *The Apprentice*. Children are set to work through mini competitions to organise the school disco. The planning of the disco is split into stages, each stage encouraging children to compete to be the person or team to have their ideas used by the judges. In my project I don't envisage the children getting fired, but I'll leave that choice up to you!

Organisation

The children need to plan a school disco to meet a budget, but also aim to make a profit. This is a real exercise: the children actually plan the school disco. All schools have discos to raise money for school funds, etc., so why not let the children organise it? First, you need to sell the idea to the current organisers of the event, usually the Parent Teacher Association (PTA), and get them on board. Having the organisers judge and play a central role will not only ensure it works but also smooth any friction that you might cause by taking a job away from someone.

When I ran this project the PTA members actually introduced the project stages in lesson time. They asked the children to organise it for them because they were 'too busy' this year.

Stage 1: Cost

The PTA came to the classroom and introduced the disco project. The children were asked to decide on the ticket price and what they wanted to sell at the disco tuck shop, as well as the budget for the fixed cost of the DJ. The PTA told the children the overall budget, how much the DJ would likely cost and what the ticket price was last year, and answered any questions. This stage started as a paper exercise in groups, each having a flip chart sheet and different coloured pens. They also had a price list from a supermarket website of sweets, drinks and snacks. The children were left to plan and later presented their ideas and costings to the class.

The second session was followed by a spreadsheet lesson where I taught the children to use simple formulas such as sum and formatting for currency. (You can see how this developed below.)

The children developed spreadsheets in pairs to allow them to calculate the cost of the disco and the profit from ticket sales. These spreadsheets would inform their final ideas to put forward to the judges. Only one idea would be taken further, but this will not be the last time the children need to use the spreadsheet.

ICT Unit 5D: Introduction to spreadsheets

Understanding and using spreadsheets is the focus for this creative project. Here is how I would introduce the concept of spreadsheets to my class.

First of all what do we know? All of the information we know and want to use needs to be on the spreadsheet and in some kind of order.

Example starting spreadsheet

a

	A	B	C	D
1	Budget	£200.00		
2				
3	Food & Drink	Unit Cost	Quantity	Total
4	Box of crisps Salt and vinegar (48 packets)	£12.67		
5	Box of crisps Cheese and Onion (48 packets)	£12.67		
6	Box of crisps Prawn Cocktail (48 packets)	£12.67		
7	Box of crisps Ready Salted (48 packets)	£12.67		
8	Box of Sweet Bananas (200)	£5.87		
9	Box of Sweet Cherries(200)	£5.87		
10	Box of mixed sweets (200)	£5.87		
11	Box of Mars Bars (48)	£11.24		
12	Box of Twix Bars (48)	£11.24		
13	Box of Malteasers (48)	£11.24		
14	Box of Fruit Pastils (48)	£11.24		
15	Box of Milky Way Bars (48)	£11.24		
16	Cans of Cola (24)	£3.99		
17	Cans of Orangeade (24)	£3.99		
18	Cans of Lemonade (24)	£3.99		
19	Cans of Cheryade (24)	£3.99		
20				
21	DJ	£120.00		
22				
23				

b

D4 f_x =C4*B4

	A	B	C	D	E
1	Budget	£250.00			
2					
3	Food & Drink	Unit Cost	Quantity	Total	
4	Box of crisps Salt and vinegar (48 packets)	£12.67		£0.00	
5	Box of crisps Cheese and Onion (48 packets)	£12.67			
6	Box of crisps Prawn Cocktail (48 packets)	£12.67			
7	Box of crisps Ready Salted (48 packets)	£12.67			
8	Box of Sweet Bananas (200)	£5.87			
9	Box of Sweet Cherries(200)	£5.87			
10	Box of mixed sweets (200)	£5.87			
11	Box of Mars Bars (48)	£11.24			
12	Box of Twix Bars (48)	£11.24			
13	Box of Malteasers (48)	£11.24			
14	Box of Fruit Pastils (48)	£11.24			
15	Box of Milky Way Bars (48)	£11.24			
16	Cans of Cola (24)	£3.99			
17	Cans of Orangeade (24)	£3.99			
18	Cans of Lemonade (24)	£3.99			
19	Cans of Cheryade (24)	£3.99			
20					
21	DJ	£120.00			
22					

c

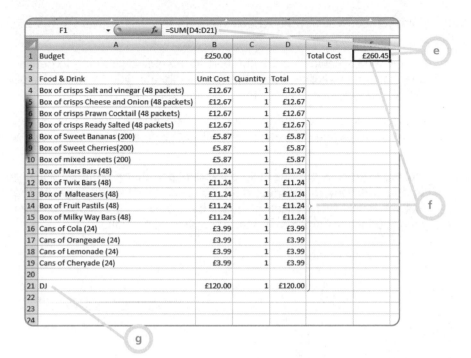

F1		▼ (	*fx* =SUM(D4:D21)		

	A	B	C	D	E	
1	Budget	£250.00			Total Cost	£260.45
2						
3	Food & Drink	Unit Cost	Quantity	Total		
4	Box of crisps Salt and vinegar (48 packets)	£12.67	1	£12.67		
5	Box of crisps Cheese and Onion (48 packets)	£12.67	1	£12.67		
6	Box of crisps Prawn Cocktail (48 packets)	£12.67	1	£12.67		
7	Box of crisps Ready Salted (48 packets)	£12.67	1	£12.67		
8	Box of Sweet Bananas (200)	£5.87	1	£5.87		
9	Box of Sweet Cherries(200)	£5.87	1	£5.87		
10	Box of mixed sweets (200)	£5.87	1	£5.87		
11	Box of Mars Bars (48)	£11.24	1	£11.24		
12	Box of Twix Bars (48)	£11.24	1	£11.24		
13	Box of Malteasers (48)	£11.24	1	£11.24		
14	Box of Fruit Pastils (48)	£11.24	1	£11.24		
15	Box of Milky Way Bars (48)	£11.24	1	£11.24		
16	Cans of Cola (24)	£3.99	1	£3.99		
17	Cans of Orangeade (24)	£3.99	1	£3.99		
18	Cans of Lemonade (24)	£3.99	1	£3.99		
19	Cans of Cheryade (24)	£3.99	1	£3.99		
20						
21	DJ	£120.00	1	£120.00		
22						
23						
24						

e

f

g

a. You can make the columns wider by clicking on the vertical divider and dragging.

b. Format cells for currency.

c. Formula for cell: =C4*B4. This allows quantity to be multiplied by unit cost.

d. Rather than type the formula repeatedly it can be copied and pasted. It will also adjust automatically.

e. Formula for cell: =SUM(D4:D21). This is the sum of the individual totals added together. This allows the quantities to be changed and the total cost will change automatically.

f. This column is added to give an overall total.

g. DJ is a cost so leave in the shop for the moment.

At this point you could survey the school. What do the children want in the shop at the disco?

Allow the children to manipulate the numbers in the quantity column to get used to the idea that the spreadsheet does the work as long as you create it carefully. The first challenge is to buy stock for the shop and keep within budget.

Once the children are happy with the stock the next step is to add the ticket price and a means of predicting how much you will make depending on the number of tickets sold.

The key to this exercise is that the children understand that a profit is needed to be successful. This early spreadsheet does not take into account that the food and drinks will be sold. The children should be left to work this out for themselves when you face the problem of the ticket price being high.

How much should we charge for tickets?

I10 f_x =I4-F1

	A	B	C	D	E	F	G	H	I	J
1	Budget	£250.00			Total Cost	£247.78		Ticket Price	£1.00	
2								Number of tickets sold	20	
3	Food & Drink	Unit Cost	Quantity	Total						
4	Box of crisps Salt and vinegar (48 packets)	£12.67	1	£12.67				Total	£20.00	
5	Box of crisps Cheese and Onion (48 packets)	£12.67	1	£12.67						
6	Box of crisps Prawn Cocktail (48 packets)	£12.67	1	£12.67						
7	Box of crisps Ready Salted (48 packets)	£12.67	0	£0.00						
8	Box of Sweet Bananas (200)	£5.87	1	£5.87						
9	Box of Sweet Cherries(200)	£5.87	1	£5.87						
10	Box of mixed sweets (200)	£5.87	1	£5.87				Profit	-£227.78	
11	Box of Mars Bars (48)	£11.24	1	£11.24						
12	Box of Twix Bars (48)	£11.24	1	£11.24						
13	Box of Malteasers (48)	£11.24	1	£11.24						
14	Box of Fruit Pastils (48)	£11.24	1	£11.24						
15	Box of Milky Way Bars (48)	£11.24	1	£11.24						
16	Cans of Cola (24)	£3.99	1	£3.99						
17	Cans of Orangeade (24)	£3.99	1	£3.99						
18	Cans of Lemonade (24)	£3.99	1	£3.99						
19	Cans of Cheryade (24)	£3.99	1	£3.99						
20										
21	DJ	£120.00	1	£120.00						
22										
23										
24										

a. Children should be encouraged to manipulate ticket price to break even. Then consider what would be a sensible price in order to generate a profit. Remember that the ticket price will be high due to the fact that the profit from selling the food and drink has not yet been considered.

b. Formula for cell: =I1*I2. The number of tickets × ticket cost.

c. Formula for cell: =I4-F1. Total cost is subtracted from ticket sales to show profit.

f   d   e

I10			fx =I4-F1								
	A	B	C	D	E	F	G	H		I	J
1	Budget	£250.00			Total Cost	£247.78		Ticket Price		£2.48	
2								Number of tickets sold		100	
3	Food & Drink	Unit Cost	Quantity	Total							
4	Box of crisps Salt and vinegar (48 packets)	£12.67	1	£12.67				Total		£248.00	
5	Box of crisps Cheese and Onion (48 packets)	£12.67	1	£12.67							
6	Box of crisps Prawn Cocktail (48 packets)	£12.67	1	£12.67							
7	Box of crisps Ready Salted (48 packets)	£12.67	0	£0.00							
8	Box of Sweet Bananas (200)	£5.87	1	£5.87							
9	Box of Sweet Cherries(200)	£5.87	1	£5.87							
10	Box of mixed sweets (200)	£5.87	1	£5.87				Profit		£0.22	
11	Box of Mars Bars (48)	£11.24	1	£11.24							
12	Box of Twix Bars (48)	£11.24	1	£11.24							
13	Box of Malteasers (48)	£11.24	1	£11.24							
14	Box of Fruit Pastils (48)	£11.24	1	£11.24							
15	Box of Milky Way Bars (48)	£11.24	1	£11.24							
16	Cans of Cola (24)	£3.99	1	£3.99							
17	Cans of Orangeade (24)	£3.99	1	£3.99							
18	Cans of Lemonade (24)	£3.99	1	£3.99							
19	Cans of Cheryade (24)	£3.99	1	£3.99							
20											
21	DJ	£120.00	1	£120.00							
22											
23											
24											
25											

d.   Remember to keep to the budget

e.   The ticket price is high and shows only 22p profit.

f.   In your preparation create your own spreadsheet in order to test the figures first – a lot will depend on the size of the budget and the number attending.

At this point it is time to make the children think for themselves, so you can test whether they understand the spreadsheet. Make a prediction based only on the money received from selling the tickets. In the above scenario tickets last year cost £1, so charging £2.50 this year is too much and people will complain. The idea that the disco will need to be cancelled because it costs too much is usually a good motivator. Try not to lead the children to an answer and do not be afraid to finish a lesson and not have an answer. If the children do not realise that the food and drink will also make a profit, and thus tickets will not need to be so expensive, get them to print out their spreadsheets and set them homework to come up with ideas to make the disco affordable.

Once the children have noticed that the shop will generate profit, you can introduce them to using more than one sheet. The idea of having a number of sheets is to help organisation. It will be much easier to work on if the shop is separate from the rest of the information, as in the figure overleaf.

Creating a separate sheet for the shop

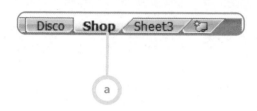

a

	A	B	C	D	E	F	G	H	I
1	Budget	£250.00			Total Cost	£260.45		Ticket Price	£1.00
2								Number of tickets sold	100
3	Food & Drink	Unit Cost	Quantity	Total					
4	Box of crisps Salt and vinegar (48 packets)	£12.67	1	£12.67				Total	£100.00
5	Box of crisps Cheese and Onion (48 packets)	£12.67	1	£12.67					
6	Box of crisps Prawn Cocktail (48 packets)	£12.67	1	£12.67					
7	Box of crisps Ready Salted (48 packets)	£12.67	1	£12.67				Profit	-£160.45
8	Box of Sweet Bananas (200)	£5.87	1	£5.87					
9	Box of Sweet Cherries(200)	£5.87	1	£5.87					
10	Box of mixed sweets (200)	£5.87	1	£5.87					
11	Box of Mars Bars (48)	£11.24	1	£11.24					
12	Box of Twix Bars (48)	£11.24	1	£11.24					
13	Box of Malteasers (48)	£11.24	1	£11.24					
14	Box of Fruit Pastils (48)	£11.24	1	£11.24					
15	Box of Milky Way Bars (48)	£11.24	1	£11.24					
16	Cans of Cola (24)	£3.99	1	£3.99					
17	Cans of Orangeade (24)	£3.99	1	£3.99					
18	Cans of Lemonade (24)	£3.99	1	£3.99					
19	Cans of Cheryade (24)	£3.99	1	£3.99					
20									
21	DJ	£120.00	1	£120.00					

D3 — Total

b

a. At the bottom of the Excel document double-click on Sheet 1 and rename it. Do the same for Sheet 2.

b. Highlight the cells containing the shop information and cut. The highlighted area will have a dotted moving line around it that looks like a row of ants.

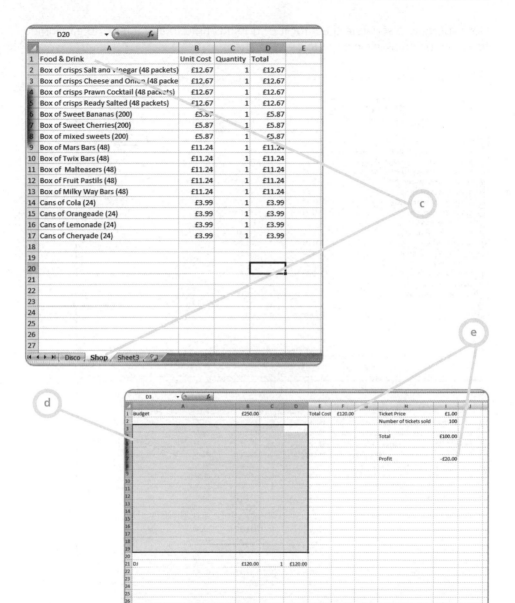

	A	B	C	D	E
1	Food & Drink	Unit Cost	Quantity	Total	
2	Box of crisps Salt and Vinegar (48 packets)	£12.67	1	£12.67	
3	Box of crisps Cheese and Onion (48 packe	£12.67	1	£12.67	
4	Box of crisps Prawn Cocktail (48 packets)	£12.67	1	£12.67	
5	Box of crisps Ready Salted (48 packets)	£12.67	1	£12.67	
6	Box of Sweet Bananas (200)	£5.87	1	£5.87	
7	Box of Sweet Cherries(200)	£5.87	1	£5.87	
8	Box of mixed sweets (200)	£5.87	1	£5.87	
9	Box of Mars Bars (48)	£11.24	1	£11.24	
10	Box of Twix Bars (48)	£11.24	1	£11.24	
11	Box of Malteasers (48)	£11.24	1	£11.24	
12	Box of Fruit Pastils (48)	£11.24	1	£11.24	
13	Box of Milky Way Bars (48)	£11.24	1	£11.24	
14	Cans of Cola (24)	£3.99	1	£3.99	
15	Cans of Orangeade (24)	£3.99	1	£3.99	
16	Cans of Lemonade (24)	£3.99	1	£3.99	
17	Cans of Cheryade (24)	£3.99	1	£3.99	

c. Click on the Shop sheet tab, click in cell A1 and paste. The information will move to the Shop sheet.

d. The Disco sheet will have an empty space where the shop contents used to be.

e. The total cost and profit will change, but leave these for now.

Now you have a separate sheet for the shop it is time to add a few more columns to allow the break-even point to be calculated.

When will the shop break even?

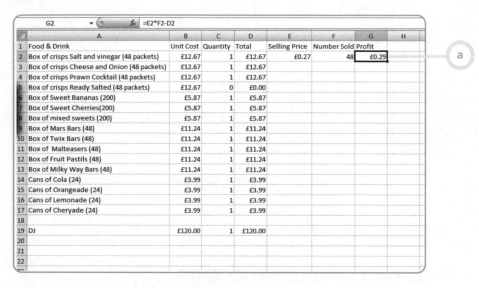

G2			f_x =E2*F2-D2					
	A	B	C	D	E	F	G	H
1	Food & Drink	Unit Cost	Quantity	Total	Selling Price	Number Sold	Profit	
2	Box of crisps Salt and vinegar (48 packets)	£12.67	1	£12.67	£0.27	48	£0.29	
3	Box of crisps Cheese and Onion (48 packets)	£12.67	1	£12.67				
4	Box of crisps Prawn Cocktail (48 packets)	£12.67	1	£12.67				
5	Box of crisps Ready Salted (48 packets)	£12.67	0	£0.00				
6	Box of Sweet Bananas (200)	£5.87	1	£5.87				
7	Box of Sweet Cherries(200)	£5.87	1	£5.87				
8	Box of mixed sweets (200)	£5.87	1	£5.87				
9	Box of Mars Bars (48)	£11.24	1	£11.24				
10	Box of Twix Bars (48)	£11.24	1	£11.24				
11	Box of Malteasers (48)	£11.24	1	£11.24				
12	Box of Fruit Pastils (48)	£11.24	1	£11.24				
13	Box of Milky Way Bars (48)	£11.24	1	£11.24				
14	Cans of Cola (24)	£3.99	1	£3.99				
15	Cans of Orangeade (24)	£3.99	1	£3.99				
16	Cans of Lemonade (24)	£3.99	1	£3.99				
17	Cans of Cheryade (24)	£3.99	1	£3.99				
18								
19	DJ	£120.00	1	£120.00				
20								
21								
22								

(a)

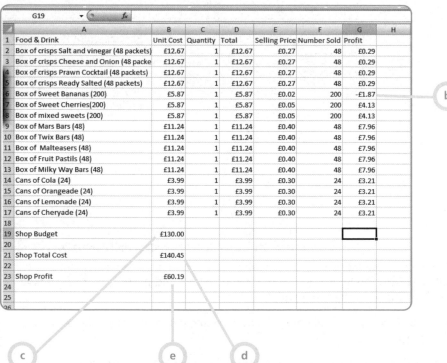

G19			f_x					
	A	B	C	D	E	F	G	H
1	Food & Drink	Unit Cost	Quantity	Total	Selling Price	Number Sold	Profit	
2	Box of crisps Salt and vinegar (48 packets)	£12.67	1	£12.67	£0.27	48	£0.29	
3	Box of crisps Cheese and Onion (48 packe	£12.67	1	£12.67	£0.27	48	£0.29	
4	Box of crisps Prawn Cocktail (48 packets)	£12.67	1	£12.67	£0.27	48	£0.29	
5	Box of crisps Ready Salted (48 packets)	£12.67	1	£12.67	£0.27	48	£0.29	
6	Box of Sweet Bananas (200)	£5.87	1	£5.87	£0.02	200	-£1.87	
7	Box of Sweet Cherries(200)	£5.87	1	£5.87	£0.05	200	£4.13	
8	Box of mixed sweets (200)	£5.87	1	£5.87	£0.05	200	£4.13	
9	Box of Mars Bars (48)	£11.24	1	£11.24	£0.40	48	£7.96	
10	Box of Twix Bars (48)	£11.24	1	£11.24	£0.40	48	£7.96	
11	Box of Malteasers (48)	£11.24	1	£11.24	£0.40	48	£7.96	
12	Box of Fruit Pastils (48)	£11.24	1	£11.24	£0.40	48	£7.96	
13	Box of Milky Way Bars (48)	£11.24	1	£11.24	£0.40	48	£7.96	
14	Cans of Cola (24)	£3.99	1	£3.99	£0.30	24	£3.21	
15	Cans of Orangeade (24)	£3.99	1	£3.99	£0.30	24	£3.21	
16	Cans of Lemonade (24)	£3.99	1	£3.99	£0.30	24	£3.21	
17	Cans of Cheryade (24)	£3.99	1	£3.99	£0.30	24	£3.21	
18								
19	Shop Budget	£130.00						
20								
21	Shop Total Cost	£140.45						
22								
23	Shop Profit	£60.19						
24								
25								
26								

(b) (c) (e) (d)

	A	B	C	D	E	F	G	H
	G20		f_x					
1	Food & Drink	Unit Cost	Quantity	Total	Selling Price	Number Sold	Profit	
2	Box of crisps Salt and vinegar (48 packets)	£12.67	1	£12.67	£0.27	48	£0.29	
3	Box of crisps Cheese and Onion (48 packe	£12.67	1	£12.67	£0.27	48	£0.29	
4	Box of crisps Prawn Cocktail (48 packets)	£12.67	1	£12.67	£0.27	48	£0.29	
5	Box of crisps Ready Salted (48 packets)	£12.67	0	£0.00	£0.00	0	£0.00	
6	Box of Sweet Bananas (200)	£5.87	1	£5.87	£0.02	200	-£1.87	
7	Box of Sweet Cherries(200)	£5.87	1	£5.87	£0.04	200	£2.13	
8	Box of mixed sweets (200)	£5.87	1	£5.87	£0.05	200	£4.13	
9	Box of Mars Bars (48)	£11.24	1	£11.24	£0.30	48	£?.??	
10	Box of Twix Bars (48)	£11.24	1	£11.24	£0.40	48	£?.??	
11	Box of Malteasers (48)	£11.24	1	£11.24	£0.50	48	£12.76	
12	Box of Fruit Pastils (48)	£11.24	1	£11.24	£0.55	48	£15.16	
13	Box of Milky Way Bars (48)	£11.24	1	£11.24	£0.60	48	£17.56	
14	Cans of Cola (24)	£3.99	1	£3.99	£0.30	24	£3.21	
15	Cans of Orangeade (24)	£3.99	1	£3.99	£0.40	24	£5.61	
16	Cans of Lemonade (24)	£3.99	1	£3.99	£0.50	24	£8.01	
17	Cans of Cheryade (24)	£3.99	1	£3.99	£0.60	24	£10.41	
18								
19	Shop Budget	£130.00						
20								
21	Shop Total Cost	£127.78						
22								
23	Shop Profit	£89.10						
24								

g

h

a. Formula for cell: =E2*F2-D2. This allows selling price to be changed and a profit for each item to be calculated. This can be copied and pasted as before.

b. Negative profit means that the selling price needs adjusting.

c. Shop is over budget. You need to buy less stock!

d. If you do allow the children to change the amounts it would be wise to add a second cell for total cost and budget.

e. Formula for cell: =SUM(G2:G17). This is the total profit made.

f. This could be a point for market research. Find out the 'going rate' for your stock. Discussions on how much to charge should be encouraged.

g. Notice that a small difference in the selling price can make a large difference in profit.

h. Formula for cell: =SUM(D2:D17). This is the total amount spent on stock.

Now the children can work out how much they want to sell their stock for. A good point to remember is that the shop may not sell everything. A discussion on how much they expect to sell and at what price, perhaps involving the PTA (or whoever ran the last disco) to offer advice or answer questions, may be helpful at this point.

Presenting the evidence

Earlier I mentioned that the front sheet is where you would keep the most important and relevant information. The final step is to make the 'disco' sheet clear and easy to understand.

The current sheet is not clear. In this figure we will change the headings to make it obvious what is being represented.

Creating a profit forecast

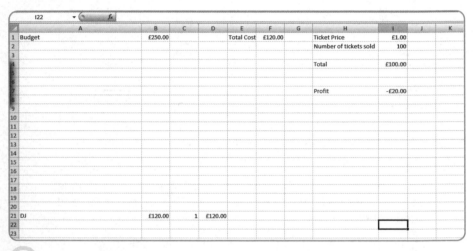

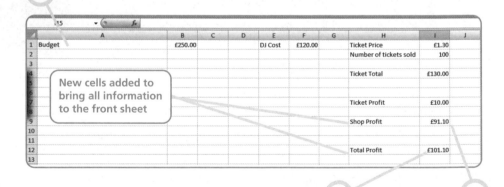

a. The Disco sheet should look something like this.

b. Cell formula: =I7+I9. This adds all predicted profit together to show a final total.

c. Cell formula: =Shop!B23. This shows the same value as the shop profit on the Shop sheet.

A finished spreadsheet may look something like the one in the next figure.

Finished spreadsheet
Sheet 1 (Disco):

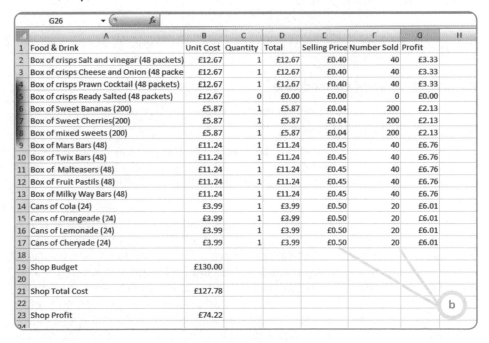

Sheet 2 (Shop):

	A	B	C	D	E	F	G	H
1	Food & Drink	Unit Cost	Quantity	Total	Selling Price	Number Sold	Profit	
2	Box of crisps Salt and vinegar (48 packets)	£12.67	1	£12.67	£0.40	40	£3.33	
3	Box of crisps Cheese and Onion (48 packe	£12.67	1	£12.67	£0.40	40	£3.33	
4	Box of crisps Prawn Cocktail (48 packets)	£12.67	1	£12.67	f0.40	40	£3.33	
5	Box of crisps Ready Salted (48 packets)	£12.67	0	£0.00	£0.00	0	£0.00	
6	Box of Sweet Bananas (200)	£5.87	1	£5.87	£0.04	200	£2.13	
7	Box of Sweet Cherries(200)	£5.87	1	£5.87	£0.04	200	£2.13	
8	Box of mixed sweets (200)	£5.87	1	£5.87	£0.04	200	£2.13	
9	Box of Mars Bars (48)	£11.24	1	£11.24	£0.45	40	£6.76	
10	Box of Twix Bars (48)	£11.24	1	£11.24	£0.45	40	£6.76	
11	Box of Malteasers (48)	£11.24	1	£11.24	£0.45	40	£6.76	
12	Box of Fruit Pastils (48)	£11.24	1	£11.24	£0.45	40	£6.76	
13	Box of Milky Way Bars (48)	£11.24	1	£11.24	£0.45	40	£6.76	
14	Cans of Cola (24)	£3.99	1	£3.99	£0.50	20	£6.01	
15	Cans of Orangeade (24)	£3.99	1	£3.99	£0.50	20	£6.01	
16	Cans of Lemonade (24)	£3.99	1	£3.99	£0.50	20	£6.01	
17	Cans of Cheryade (24)	£3.99	1	£3.99	£0.50	20	£6.01	
18								
19	Shop Budget	£130.00						
20								
21	Shop Total Cost	£127.78						
22								b
23	Shop Profit	£74.22						

a. To make text visible in cell, right-click, select Format Cell from the drop-down menu, then in the Alignment tab select Wrap Text.

b. Here you can see the prices I decided on and the predicted numbers I expect to sell.

Stage 2: Advertising and tickets

Note: This stage could be planned in literacy. Although there is no specific ICT unit focus, allowing the children to choose the software and media they use can give you a good overview of their ICT skills.

Again this stage was introduced by the PTA. They told the children they needed tickets and posters designing and that they were to be printed by our local City Learning Centre. They needed to show the price, date and start and finish times, and have a title or slogan that was catchy. There had to be two A1 posters for the hall and entrance hall, eight A3 posters for every exit the children use, and 20 A4 posters for putting up around the school. The only restriction was that it needed to be emailed to the City Learning Centre for printing.

This was an open-ended team task. I gave the children an afternoon. They had use of the ICT suite, paint, paper, cameras and anything they could think of (within reason). At the end of the afternoon the entries would be judged by the PTA and the children would know which team's poster would be used. The posters were made, judged and the children went home, while I promised to email the posters to the printers.

Stage 3: Oh no!

ICT Unit 6B: Spreadsheet modelling

(*Note*: This section is not a replacement for this unit but could be looked back upon or incorporated at the beginning).

The children arrived the next day to be greeted by the printing bill from the City Learning Centre on the whiteboard (£30). When I was finally asked what it was (it took some time) I explained and asked them if they had budgeted for it. I obviously knew the answer.

The next lesson took us back to the winning spreadsheet to find a way of adding the new expense whilst still keeping under budget. The only place we could cut back was from the shop (unless we don't have a DJ!) or we could raise the ticket price … but they were already printed. Something had to go, but what? The children worked in different pairs than before and discussed what stock they would remove from the shop. There was a twist. I had arranged for the school secretary to interrupt with a message from the PTA about halfway through the lesson. The PTA had found some more money and could give us an extra £15. The spreadsheets had to change again. Our secretary returned once more 10 minutes later to tell us that the City Learning Centre had overcharged us. The bill was actually £20.

The spreadsheets had taken a severe pounding and as a class we decided which option to take to recover the £5. We eventually took out a box of cheaper sweets as they made the least profit.

Changing the spreadsheet

	A	B	C	D	E	F	G	H	I
	122							f_x	
1	Budget	£250.00			DJ Cost	£120.00		Ticket Price	£1.50
2								Number of tickets sold	325
3									
4								Ticket Total	£487.50
5	My prediction is based on the whole school attending and all of the cheaper sweets, most of the crisps, chocolate and drinks being sold. If all of the stock sold the profit would be £477.32								
6									
7								Ticket Profit	£367.50
8									
9								Shop Profit	£74.22
10									
11									
12								Total Profit	£441.72
13									
14									
15	Shop Costs	£127.78							
16	DJ Costs	£120.00							
17	Printing Costs	£30.00							
18									
19	Total Costs	£277.78							
20									

b   a

a. At first there is a need to save £30.

b. Currently £27.78 over budget. The children must meet the budget by changing the amount of stock bought for the shop.

Stage 4: Where will it go?

ICT Unit 5A: Graphical modelling

This is the perfect opportunity to use mathematics. The children need to measure and produce a scale drawing of the perimeter of the hall. Next they have to fit all of the disco equipment, tuck shop, seating, etc. into the drawing (also to scale). In doing this the children will be given the opportunity to 'progress further':

'Children who progress further will use an object-based graphics package to create and explore an accurate graphical model checking predictions and make decisions.'

(QCA ICT Unit 5A, 1998)

The chair of the PTA came to visit the class and asked them to decide where everything will go. The DJ and parents who were going to run the shop needed a floor plan. It had to be safe, wires could not be trailing to the disco and the exits needed to be clear and there had to be an area to sit if you wanted to eat, drink or rest.

The children needed to draw a scale plan of the hall and arrange everything to meet the criteria. This was an individual project done in Word using the grid guides to generate the scale. Other programs could be used but using Word saved having to teach the children how to use additional software in a short time. This was again judged by the PTA and used to set up the hall on the night.

Using the grid guides in Word 2007

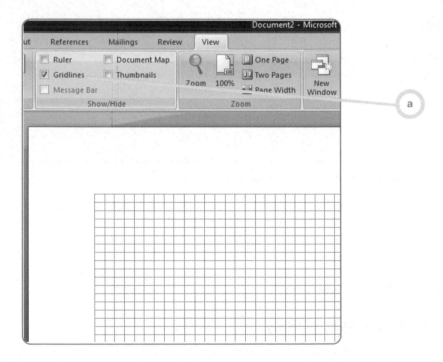

a. In the View menu click Gridlines.

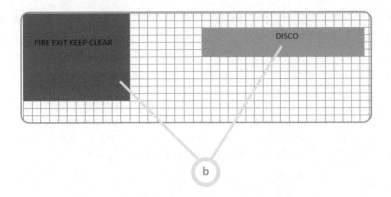

b. If you use text boxes for the simple shapes it is easy to add a label.

Stage 5: Health and safety

ICT Unit 6A: Multimedia presentations

This again allows the children to meet the 'children who progress further' target:

'Use a multimedia package to organise, refine and present a set of linked multimedia pages, which incorporate images, sounds and text; create pages which offer users a variety of options; present information that matches the needs of the audience.'

(QCA ICT Unit 6A: Multimedia presentations, 1998)

The PTA returned again. They needed a presentation to be made on health and safety at the school disco for every class. It needed to be memorable, have animation and some sounds but, most importantly, get the message across. The children were put into teams to plan and then present. There would be a need to consider the audience as KS1 and KS2 would have to be differentiated. Each group was allocated a class in the school they were to present to and together we developed the content that needed to be in the presentation. The children chose to use PowerPoint for this because they were presenting in person but Photo Story 3 would also be suitable.

Stage 6: Profit and evaluation

After the disco the PTA came to thank the children for their hard work and told them how much profit they had made. They also introduced the evaluation in the form of writing a letter to next year's children telling them what to look out for and any advice they would give them.

This project worked because it was guaranteed to work. Children were always going to go to the disco, and although all my class did was order some sweets, print posters and move some furniture around, they took it seriously because it was theirs. The fact that the PTA trusted them with the budget, asked them to plan and then followed what the children requested made it real. When the children finally made a profit they were over the moon and straight away asked if they could plan the next disco. I told them I'd think about it!

Conclusion

As a teacher you are considered to be an expert in education. You would never buy a scheme of work for any other subject simply on the word of the salesperson, and you would never restock your library with the recommended reading list from one publisher, yet with ICT many schools entrust one company with thousands of pounds to change their infrastructure, then, once everything is installed, involve and train their staff.

I believe it is time for teachers to take charge of their use of ICT, question the educational value of what they are currently using and rigorously test what they will be using in the future. After reading this book, I hope you will feel more confident to question any technology you do not deem to be of educational value to your pupils. In the end, in your school and certainly in your classroom, you know your pupils better than anyone. You are the expert.

Glossary

Clipboard memory Where anything that is cut or copied is stored. This memory usually only holds one item at any given time.

Copy Copies a previously highlighted text object or picture (it will not disappear from the work area) so you can paste it again as many times as you like until you cut or copy something else.

Cut Cuts a previously highlighted text object or picture out (so you won't see it any more) and holds it in the clipboard memory. It will stay there and can be pasted as many times as you like until you cut or copy something else (it only holds one thing at a time).

Dongle A small peripheral device that usually has a USB connection. Most commonly a storage device.

Drive A device that can store data.

Ethernet cable In school this connects you to the internet, your network or both.

FireWire A cable that allows peripheral devices to communicate with your computer.

Highlight (or highlighting) is when you left-click with the mouse (hold) and drag. A coloured block will form as you pass over text and pictures will also change colour. Anything that is surrounded by the new colour can be considered highlighted and can be cut or copied (you can usually always copy, but some programs, e.g. pages on the internet and acrobat reader, can not be cut).

Hyperlink A link to the internet, see Chapter 2.

Interactive whiteboard Any surface that allows interaction with a computer and the software installed on it.

Jack A cylindrical plug connection usually associated with audio or charging connections, used to connect both microphones and headphones to the computer.

Parallel pin There connections have been superseded by USB and other connections but can still be found on older devices.

Paste Pastes what you have cut or copied wherever you have selected.

Pen drives Another name for USB storage devices.

Peripheral devices These are devices that can be added to your computer, e.g. cameras, printers, etc.

Screen capture (Ctrl+Prtsc) allows an image of the screen to be taken to the clipboard (computer memory). Some interactive whiteboard software allows sections of the screen to be captured.

SD card A Secure Digital card used to store data such as images in a digital camera.

Search engines find information on the internet usually by matching words. Such searches can be filtered for greater accuracy.

Sound sockets The female connection for the jack plug. On most computers they are colour coded and most commonly accept a microphone, headphones or speakers.

Taskbar The bar at the bottom of the screen that allows you to switch between programs, see Chapter 2.

USB cable (Universal Serial Bus) A cable that allows a number of different peripheral devices to connect in a standardised way.

VGA (Video Graphics Array) cables allow the display on your screen to be shown elsewhere.

Wireless connection/networks communicate without the use of wires (like the radio in a car).

Wizards guide you through the project you are creating giving instructions or automatically completing sections for you.

Index

Classroom Gems

Innovative resources, inspiring creativity across the school curriculum

Designed with busy teachers in mind, the Classroom Gems series draws together an extensive selection of practical, tried-and-tested, off-the-shelf ideas, games and activities, guaranteed to transform any lesson or classroom in an instant.

Games and activities for
Primary Modern Foreign Languages
Maria Greenacre

© 2008 Paperback 336pp
ISBN: 9781405873925

Practical ideas, games and activities for the
Primary Classroom
Paul Barron

© 2008 Paperback 312pp
ISBN: 9781405859455

Games, ideas and activities for
Primary PE
Will Allen

© 2009 Paperback 224pp
ISBN: 9781408220382

Games, ideas and activities for
Learning Outside the Primary Classroom
Paul Barron

© 2009 Paperback 256pp
ISBN: 9781408225608

Games, ideas and activities for
Primary Mathematics
John Dabell

© 2009 Paperback 304pp
ISBN: 9781408223208

Games, ideas and activities for
Primary Humanities
Richard Green

© 2009 Paperback 304pp
ISBN: 9781408228098

Games, ideas and activities for
Primary Music
Donna Minto

© 2009 Paperback 304pp
ISBN: 9781408223260

Games, ideas and activities for
Primary Drama
Michael Theodorou

© 2009 Paperback 304pp
ISBN: 9781408223291

Games, ideas and activities for
Early Years Phonics
Lynn Cousins and Gill Coulson

© 2009 Paperback 304pp
ISBN: 9781408224359

Creative activities for the
Secondary Classroom
Mark Labrow

© 2009 Paperback 256pp
ISBN: 9781408225578

Games, ideas and activities for
Primary Science
John Dabell

© 2010 Paperback 304pp
ISBN: 9781408223239

Games, ideas and activities for
Primary Literacy
Hazel Glynne and Amanda Snowden

© 2010 Paperback 336pp
ISBN: 9781408225516

'Easily navigable, allowing teachers to choose the right activity quickly and easily, these invaluable resources are guaranteed to save time and are a must-have tool to plan, prepare and deliver first-rate lessons'

Longman
is an imprint of

PEARSON

The Essential Guides Series

Practical skills for teachers

The Essential Guides series offers a wealth of practical support, inspiration and guidance for NQTs and more experienced teachers ready to implement into their classroom. The books provide practical advice and tips on the core aspects of teaching and everyday classroom issues, such as planning, assessment, behaviour and ICT. The Essential Guides are invaluable resources that will help teachers to successfully navigate the challenges of the profession.

The Essential Guide to
Successful School Trips
John Trant

© 2010 paperback
ISBN 978-1-4082-0447-4

The Essential Guide to
Shaping Children's Behaviour in the Early Years
Lynn Cousins

© 2010 paperback
ISBN 978-1-4082-2502-8

The Essential Guide to
Secondary Teaching
Susan Davies

© 2010 paperback ISBN 978-1-4082-2452-6

The Essential Guide to
Classroom Assessment
Paul Dix

© 2010 paperback
ISBN 978-1-4082-3025-1

The Essential Guide to
Taking Care of Behaviour
(second edition)
Paul Dix

© 2010 paperback
ISBN 978-1-4082-2554-7

The Essential Guide to
Teaching 14-19 Diplomas
Lynn Senior

© 2010 paperback
ISBN 978-1-4082-2549-3

The Essential Guide to
Understanding Special Educational Needs
Jenny Thompson

© 2010 paperback
ISBN 978-1-4082-2500-4

Longman
is an imprint of

PEARSON

Practical skills for teachers